# HOW TO SUCCEED AT AN ASSESSMENT CENTRE

# HOW TO SUCCEED AT AN ASSESSMENT CENTRE

Essential preparation for psychometric tests, group and role-play exercises, panel interviews and presentations

3rd edition

HARRY TOLLEY
ROBERT WOOD

KOGAN PAGE

**Publisher's Note**

Every possible effort has been made to ensure that the information contained in this book is accurate at the time of going to press, and the publishers and authors cannot accept responsibility for any errors or omissions, however caused. No responsibility for loss or damage occasioned to any person acting, or refraining from action, as a result of the material in this publication can be accepted by the editor, the publisher or any of the authors.



**First Indian Edition 2010**



**Kogan Page India Private Limited**
4737/23 Ansari Road,
Daryaganj
New Delhi 110 002

*This edition is for sale in the Indian subcontinent only. Not for export elsewhere.*

ISBN: 978-81-7554-504-5

Published by Vinod Vasishtha for Kogan Page India Private Limited,
4737/23 Ansari Road, Daryaganj, New Delhi - 110 002.

Printed and bound at Raj Press, R-3, Inderpuri, New Delhi - 110 012.

# Contents

# About the authors

Dr Harry Tolley is a Special Professor in the School of Education at the University of Nottingham as well as being a researcher, author and freelance consultant. He is the co-author of *How to Pass Numeracy Tests, How to Pass Verbal Reasoning Tests* and *How to Pass the New Police Selection System*, all published by Kogan Page.

Professor Robert Wood is an author and freelance consultant. He has written and co-written numerous books and papers based on his extensive experience in recruitment, assessment and selection. He now writes novels, short stories and walking books.

# Introduction

It has been common practice to invite candidates who have successfully negotiated a job or a promotion interview to attend for a second interview. This was often very similar to the first, though the chances are that the questions would have been more searching, and the candidates would have had to face a panel rather than a single interviewer. However, many organizations have now come to realize that such procedures are seriously flawed as a means of recruiting new people, or even as a method of selecting employees for promotion or further training. The reasons for this are:

- A second interview can easily cover the same issues in a similar way to the first – even when conducted by skilled and experienced interviewers.
- Selection based purely on interviews is likely to be more subjective than is desirable because of the importance attached to first impressions, and the possibility of stereotyping and unintended bias on the part of the interviewers.
- Interviews on their own do not provide organizations with sufficient information about the ability of candidates to cope with the particular requirements of the job, course of training or education programme for which they have applied.

Consequently, there are serious doubts about both the validity and reliability of interviews as the *sole* means of selecting people for whatever purpose. Some time ago, one recruitment specialist summed this up as follows: 'It is probably the worst way to recruit. You may as well just toss a coin' (Angela Baron, Chartered Institute of Personnel and Development, cited in an article in *Daily Telegraph Business File*, 29 April 1999).

Nevertheless, the emphasis is on the word 'sole' – because you must still expect to be interviewed at some point in the selection process. For example, you might be invited to participate in a 'telephone interview' during which a potential employer asks you to elaborate on the information you have provided in your written application. This also provides recruiters with an opportunity to assess your oral communication when using the telephone – skills which are of particular importance in jobs such as market research, telephone sales, customer care and those at call centres. Alternatively, you might be given an opportunity early in the employment process (eg at a recruitment fair) to take part in what is known as a 'speed interview'. This is not a substitute for a formal, in-depth interview. It is simply a quick and easy way of helping potential candidates and recruiters to decide if they are attracted by what each other has to offer.

So, after such an experience you might decide to apply for organizations A and B rather than any of the other options open to you. You will then enter into the full selection process, which is likely at some point to include a 'traditional interview' – still seen by many recruiters as being a low-risk, tried and tested method of selecting personnel.

However, in the interests of efficiency and cost-effectiveness, organizations are now seeking to select staff who have the competencies and personal attributes that match the precise needs of the job or the demands of the course of training and/or education programme for which they have applied. They have concluded, therefore, that the more information they have about the ability, personality and behaviour of candidates the more they reduce the chances of making the costly mistake of appointing, promoting or selecting someone who is unsuitable. Thus, more and more of the applicants for jobs, promotion, further training and even education courses can now expect to be assessed by a variety of methods in a recruitment-selection process, which consists of a number of stages.

For the candidate, this is a multi-stage assessment process usually beginning with the completion and submission of some form of written application – an on-line application form, a curriculum vitae and/or a letter. These will not only be used as an initial filter, ie to decide whether or not to progress your application to the next stage in the recruitment process, but also to build up the evidence on which the final assessment of your suitability will be based. What you submit can also be used to inform subsequent stages in the assessment process, eg the questions for you to be asked in an interview, or what behaviours to look out for when you are interacting with other people. It is worth remembering that in completing this stage of the process, you will be judged not just on the content of your application, but also on your written communication skills including the accuracy of your spelling, punctuation and grammar. Given the importance of 'first impressions' in a highly competitive labour market, you cannot afford to treat this initial stage of the process lightly, and we strongly recommend that you read and follow the advice given in the other books in the Kogan Page series written specifically for this purpose, such as *Preparing the Perfect Job Application* and *Preparing the Perfect CV*.

Candidates judged to best meet the selection criteria in the early stages of the process are now likely to find themselves invited to attend what is known as an 'assessment centre', where further evaluation of their suitability will be undertaken over an extended period of time – sometimes several hours, sometimes even longer. It should be noted that in this context the term 'assessment centre' refers to a process rather than a location – a term like 'multi-assessment event' would do just as well.

Assessment centres are highly structured in terms of both their programmes and assessment activities – the same being true of multi-assessment events. They will be run, in some cases, by human resources staff from within the organization, assisted, as appropriate, by other people such as senior managers. In other situations, recruitment professionals such as occupational psychologists from outside the organization may be involved as consultants, and actors may be employed in some role-play activities.

The structure and content of the programme will vary according to the precise details of the job or training opportunity on offer. For example, a post in management might involve a combination of the following activities: an in-tray or 'in-box' exercise; group problem solving; a case study; presentations; ability tests; and personality inventories/questionnaires. For jobs in other types of employment there may well be a greater emphasis on, for example, creative thinking, information technology (IT), numeracy or written communication skills.

Whatever the selection of activities, the emphasis is often on the observable behaviour of candidates, and to that end exercises will have been designed to capture and simulate key aspects of the relevant job. For example, would-be police officers are required to participate in role-play exercises in which they have to deal with problem situations. The candidates' performance on tasks such as these is then assessed against criteria derived from the competencies required for the job.

Unfortunately, many good candidates fail to do themselves justice because they are unaware of what kinds of tasks they may be asked to undertake when attending an assessment centre or multi-assessment event. The **aims** of this book, therefore, are to:

- inform you about what to expect when you are asked to attend an assessment event of this kind;
- explain how such events are conducted and how this fits into the whole recruitment and selection process;
- offer advice on how you should behave during your time at an assessment centre in both formal and informal situations;
- give guidance on how you might prepare for the different forms of assessment (including ability and other tests) you are likely to face in order to maximize your chances of success;
- suggest learning activities that you can undertake in order to prepare yourself for the different types of assessment exercises you are likely to face.

The contents of this book and the way they have been organized and presented are designed to help you to achieve these goals. As this is the third edition of the book, we have taken advantage of the opportunity to update its content, most noticeably by adding new material to existing chapters. As a result, the book more accurately reflects recent developments and trends in the ways in which assessment centres and multi-assessment events are conducted. We begin in **Chapter 1** by giving you an introduction to what to expect if you are invited to attend an assessment event of this kind.

1

# Assessment centres and multi-assessment events

In this chapter you will be given an overview of what to expect if you are invited to attend an assessment centre or to participate in a multi-assessment event. We will therefore explain to you: what an assessment centre is; what kind of programme to expect; and the assessment exercises you are likely to encounter. In addition, we will give you constructive guidance on how to cope with the demands that will be placed upon you, and how you should prepare for attending an assessment centre. The chapter also deals with those aspects of the assessment centre experience which often cause participants trouble, such as the social activities included in the programme, dress codes and punctuality. Finally, we offer guidance on some of the things you can do to prepare for attending an assessment centre or multi-assessment event.

## What is an assessment centre?

If you are invited to attend an assessment centre, you will join a small group of other applicants, possibly as many as a dozen. Together you will be asked to undertake a series of assessments that have been designed to reveal to the assessors whether you possess the competencies and personal attributes necessary for you to: work effectively in the relevant job; benefit from a further training opportunity; or cope with the demands of an education programme.

Depending on the arrangements, the assessment process can take anything from a few hours to a couple of days. In the latter case, both the candidates and the assessors are likely to be in residence at the same place. It is not surprising, therefore, that some candidates find this to be quite stressful, not least because they are in an unfamiliar environment with people who are strangers to them, doing something to which they are not accustomed. It is natural for those who find themselves in this position to have trouble relaxing because they think that they are being assessed all the time – even during informal breaks in the proceedings. What you must always remember is that, because of the expense entailed, organizations will only invite those candidates to an assessment centre or a multi-assessment event they consider to be worthy of closer scrutiny. This means that, if you have got through to this stage in the recruitment selection process, you must be getting closer to being one of the chosen candidates. If you are not yet on the 'short list' of those from whom the final selection will be made, you are certainly on the 'long list'!

## What to expect – the programme

If you are fortunate enough to receive an invitation to attend a multi-assessment event, what should you expect? The letter inviting you to attend should give you a good idea. First, it should provide you with details concerning the venue itself – the address, location and how to get there. Then you should be given some preliminary information about what to expect, including an outline of the programme together with the approximate timings. Under normal circumstances you should also be given an indication of the types of assessment that will be used and their place and purpose in the overall selection process. Some organizations may even send you some sample test items as an aid to your preparation, together with a questionnaire to complete. What this information should signal to you is that your time at an assessment centre or a multi-assessment event will be structured and highly organized. This can be illustrated by reference to the sample timetables given in **Figures 1.1** to **1.3** – one for a half-day event (**Figure 1.1**), one for a one-day programme (**Figure 1.2**) and the other for two days (**Figure 1.3**).

These sample timetables are intended to show what you might expect if you are invited to an assessment centre – though, when studying these timetables, you need to bear in mind that there are no hard-and-fast rules about how such programmes should be compiled. Consequently, there are many

| | |
|---|---|
| **13.00** | Arrive, welcome and introductions |
| **13.15** | Cognitive test (critical thinking) |
| **14.00** | Group discussion exercise |
| **14.45** | Break |
| **15.00** | Presentations |
| **16.00** | Interviews |
| **17.00** | Debriefing |
| **17.30** | Depart |

**Figure 1.1** Sample timetable for a half-day multi-assessment event

| | |
|---|---|
| **10.00** | Arrive, registration, coffee |
| **10.15** | Welcome and introductions |
| **10.30** | Cognitive and personality tests |
| **12.30** | Buffet lunch with departmental staff |
| **13.45** | Interviews* |
| **15.00** | Break |
| **15.15** | Group discussion exercise |
| **16.30** | Debriefing |
| **17.00** | Depart |

* Applicants who do not do well enough on the tests may be asked to leave following a short feedback session

**Figure 1.2** Sample timetable for a one-day assessment centre

**DAY 1**

| | |
|---|---|
| **17.00** | Arrive at venue for the assessment centre (eg a hotel) |
| **18.00** | Welcome and introductory briefing |
| **18.30** | Icebreaker activity |
| **20.00** | Dinner with representatives from the organization and assessors<br>Work on preparatory task for following day's activities (eg complete a questionnaire, read documents provided) |

**DAY 2**

| | |
|---|---|
| **09.00** | Introduction to the day's programme |
| **09.15** | Cognitive test and personality inventory |
| **11.00** | Coffee |
| **11.15** | In-tray or in-box exercise |
| **12.15** | Presentations |
| **13.00** | Lunch with senior managers and assessors |
| **14.00** | Group decision-making exercise |
| **15.00** | Break |
| **15.15** | Interviews |
| **16.15** | Debriefing session and brief presentation of the organization's training and development programme |
| **17.00** | Finish and depart |

**Figure 1.3** Sample timetable for a two-day assessment centre

variants depending upon the circumstances. For example, would-be police officers are required to attend a multi-assessment event that lasts for approximately four hours, during which they are given an interview, undertake a writing exercise, take two psychometric tests and participate in role-plays – though not necessarily in that order. So, if you want to know exactly what to expect, you will need to take a careful look at the timetable you have been given.

What the sample programmes also show is how busy you can expect to be during the time you are in attendance. Indeed, as a candidate, you will find that there will be very little time when you are not actively engaged in one form of assessment or another. All of this variety and intensity of activity is intended to do more than simply provide the assessors with as much evidence as possible about the applicants in the shortest possible time. Part of its purpose is to observe at first hand how you behave under pressure by simulating the circumstances under which you might be expected to perform in a real work-place, such as dealing with a difficult customer, working together in a team or handling electronic communication efficiently. In turn, the variety of assessment tasks is intended to provide different forms of evidence about you and the other candidates. This will then enable the assessors to build up a profile of you and the other candidates based on your performance on the individual assessment items. The completed profiles can then be used when making the final decision.

In short, the principles that underpin the conduct of this form of assessment are that the evidence on which the final decisions are made should have been: derived from a range of carefully chosen tasks; and based upon the judgements of more than one assessor. Only by following these principles can the reliability and validity of the final outcomes be boosted to desirable levels.

## What to expect – the assessment activities

As with the programme, there is no set formula as to how many exercises or which combination of activities should be included in an assessment centre or multi-assessment event. This is because the assessment tasks will have been chosen to provide the assessors with evidence of the extent to which the candidates possess those competencies judged to be relevant to the particular job, development opportunity or programme of study under consideration. However, the research findings, which are summarized in **Table 1.1**, tell us that certain types of exercise are more likely to occur at an assessment centre than others, irrespective of the size of the recruiting organization. For example, as the table shows, assessment centres are almost certain to include some form of interview (ie one to one or by an interview panel). What is crucial is that this is not the sole method of extracting behavioural evidence. Other methods will comprise some or all of the following: an aptitude (ability) test; a personality questionnaire; a group discussion exercise; perhaps a case study; a presentation; and an in-tray/in-box exercise. That is to say, in any assessment programme you should expect to encounter a combination of some of the following assessment tasks:

- one-to-one interview or a panel interview;
- ability tests (sometimes known as 'cognitive' or 'psychometric' tests);
- personality questionnaires (or 'inventories');
- group discussion exercise;
- case study;
- in-tray/in-box exercise;
- presentation.

**Table 1.1** Content of assessment centre exercises in the UK according to size of recruiting organizations (small, medium, large)

| Type of exercise | Small (%) | Medium (%) | Large (%) | Total sample (%) |
|---|---|---|---|---|
| Interview | 97 | 97 | 97 | 97 |
| Aptitude test | 89 | 91 | 91 | 91 |
| Personality test | 80 | 83 | 79 | 80 |
| Group discussion | 67 | 79 | 89 | 79 |
| Case study | 49 | 64 | 71 | 62 |
| Presentation | 54 | 59 | 61 | 58 |
| In-tray/in-box | 19 | 38 | 48 | 35 |

By way of giving you an overview of what to expect, a brief description is provided below for each of the most common types of assessment tasks. More detailed guidance on what is involved and how you can best prepare for them is then given in the subsequent chapters of this book.

## Interviews

An interview is an interview; we all think we know what to expect. You may already have had some form of an interview prior to your receiving an invitation to attend an assessment centre and now you are to be interviewed again. However, you would be well advised to approach this so-called 'second interview' with greater care and prepare for it more thoroughly than you might have done ahead of the first interview. This is not just because the stakes get higher the closer you get to the point at which the final selection is made: second interviews tend to be more challenging, perhaps because the assessors are just a little more on their mettle.

So, in what ways do assessment centre interviews differ from first interviews? The main features of second interviews are that they are:

- often conducted by a panel drawn from senior managers, staff with relevant professional or technical expertise, human resource personnel and even outside consultants;
- driven by highly specific selection criteria, and as such are intended to provide evidence that complements evidence obtained by other means;
- based on more searching questions, which may be informed by how you have performed on the other assessment exercises or information you have provided in your application;
- likely to focus at some point on any issues that were raised during your first interview and that need further exploration.

In the light of this knowledge it is worth doing a little advance preparation before you go to the assessment centre. As you can see from the sample timetables given in **Figures 1.1** to **1.3**, the chances are that you won't have much time when you get there. A checklist of useful things that you can do to get started on that process is given in the box below.

To sum up, expect your assessment centre interview to be more demanding than the one that helped to get you there, make sure you are familiar with what you said in your

You can prepare in advance for your assessment centre interview by:

- taking a careful look at the job details together with your initial application, CV and covering letter and reflecting on them in the light of the knowledge you have since gained;
- studying any notes you made following your first interview;
- thinking about what questions you were asked at that interview and whether or not any areas were left unexplored;
- trying to identify what new questions you might be asked or areas the interviewers might wish to explore;
- gathering relevant information about the organization, eg from someone you know who may have had a second interview or via the internet.

application form, CV and supporting letter, and find out as much as you can about the job and the organization. More detailed guidance is given in **Chapter 6**.

## Ability tests

The use of tests in personnel selection is based on the assumption that there are stable job-related differences between candidates, and that these differences can be measured with a sufficient degree of accuracy to be of value to employers. The ability tests chosen for use at an assessment centre, therefore, will have been specifically designed to assess how good people are at doing certain things. So, expect to be given a test or tests that will provide the assessors with some objective evidence of what you are able to do – in other words, a measure of your aptitude.

The most commonly used ability tests are designed to assess your skills in numeracy and verbal reasoning. In addition there are tests that can be used to assess critical thinking, problem solving, technical skills, spatial reasoning and situational judgement. Hence, any cognitive tests that are used at an assessment centre will have been carefully chosen to provide evidence of the skills and abilities you possess that are relevant to the job, training opportunity or programme of study under consideration. That evidence will then be considered alongside the outcomes from the other assessment exercises in arriving at the final selection. For you, the candidate, that is the beauty of multi-assessment events and assessment centres – the result does not hinge solely on your performance on just one assessment task. Always remember this, especially if you are struggling with one of the exercises.

To sum up, nearly all recruiters make use of some form of ability test at an assessment centre in order to measure the aptitude of candidates – the choice of which tests to use being closely related to the abilities judged to be relevant to the job,

You should know the following about ability tests:

- They invariably begin with one or two worked examples to introduce you to what is involved and inform you about how to proceed.
- There are strict time limits for each test, designed in such a way as to put you under time pressure – so much so that you may not be able to complete all of the questions.
- The answers to the items will be either correct or incorrect.
- The items may be arranged within the test on a 'gradient of difficulty', with the easiest questions at the beginning and the hardest at the end.
- They may be in the form of a 'paper-and-pencil' test or you may be asked to answer questions online, which is a growing trend.

training opportunity or place on an education course that is on offer. More detailed guidance is provided in **Chapter 4.**

## Personality questionnaires

Personality questionnaires, sometimes called 'inventories', are designed to measure such personal characteristics or 'traits' as your motivation to work and how you handle your emotions. Indeed with regard to the latter you may be asked to complete what is known as an emotional intelligence (EI) test or emotional intelligence inventory. The information which these instruments provide is of great interest to prospective employers because it provides a basis for predicting how your individual personality is likely to affect your future performance. It may be important, for example, for them to know if you are the kind of person who can stay calm but alert in the conditions that prevail in a particular workplace, or have the ability to adapt to the culture of their organization. Evidence from personality questionnaires, along with that derived from ability tests and other forms of assessment, therefore, is used to help choose the people who are best suited for the job or would benefit most from further training or an education programme.

The most common features of personality inventories used at assessment centres are as follows:

- They usually start with one or two sample items, which give you an idea as to what is involved and how to proceed.
- Though time pressure is less important than it is with ability tests, you will usually be given a fixed time in which to complete the inventory.
- Unlike ability tests there are no correct or incorrect answers – you are usually expected to rate yourself on some sort of scale.
- They usually include some items that check whether or not you are trying to give a false impression of yourself by answering untruthfully and inconsistently.
- They may be in 'paper-and-pencil' form or you may be required to complete them online – as with ability tests and in-box exercises, this is a growing trend.
- The answers given are used to construct individual personality or EI profiles.

To sum up, you should expect aspects of your personality and emotional intelligence to be evaluated in some way or another at an assessment centre or a multi-assessment event. To that end it will help your cause greatly if you know yourself well, are prepared to be honest and are aware of the personal qualities required. More detailed guidance is given in **Chapter 5**.

## Group exercises

Group exercises require you to interact with others in prearranged ways in order that the assessors can observe and evaluate your behaviour. The group exercises used at an assessment centre fall into three main categories: group discussions; problem solving; and team games. Discussion groups include:

- leaderless discussion, in which all of the participants are given the same brief and are expected to work towards achieving a consensus;
- discussions in which each member of the group is given the opportunity (eg 10 minutes) to chair the proceedings;
- discussion where each of the participants is presented with a different brief in which they are assigned a role they are expected to play in the subsequent interactions of the group.

In the case of problem-solving exercises, you should expect to be given a task which requires your group to work together to find a solution to a problem. This can take the form of an abstract problem, or be based on case study material (see below), which requires decision making (or 'situational judgements') based on concrete material derived from a specific context, which may be either real or hypothetical.

Team games are another variant of group exercises. Typically, you will be a member of a team that is given a common task to complete in competition with another team or against the clock. It is common in exercises such as this for the group to be given a collection of basic materials such as newspaper, string and sticky tape, or a construction kit, which they are instructed to use to build something such as a tower or a bridge. Under this heading you should also be prepared for role-playing exercises in which you may be asked to act the part of a character, usually in a work-related context. For example, would-be police officers may be asked to deal with a highly distressed person who has lost something valuable, or a colleague who has been the subject of racist or sexist comments.

In exercises such as these the assessors will be looking for behavioural evidence of, for example, your:

- ability to participate in the group's activities and to make a positive contribution to achieving its goals;
- listening skills;

- oral communication skills including your ability to present reasoned arguments;
- negotiation and assertiveness skills;
- ability to work effectively in a group including your interpersonal skills and ability to empathize with others;
- leadership skills.

To sum up, there is a very good chance that you will be involved in some form of group discussion and/or role-play activity at an assessment centre or multi-assessment event, especially those run on behalf of large organizations. You should expect these to take many different forms, but in each case it will be your observable behaviour that will be of interest to the assessors. For further guidance see **Chapter 2** and **Chapter 7**.

## Case study

The most common form of a case study used at assessment centres is a business or technical problem that has been chosen because it is both realistic and relevant to the job on offer. You will be given information relevant to the problem, and be required to work with others in a group. In such cases the exercise will be a variant of the group exercises described above. As such it may be that it is not only the solution to the problem that will be of interest to the assessors, but how it was arrived at and the contributions you made to that process. Thus, a case study is normally used as a vehicle for generating a wide range of activities in order to provide the assessors with evidence of your oral communication and team-working skills as well as your ability to:

- analyse issues embedded in the case study materials;
- interpret data presented in a variety of forms;
- consider alternative solutions to the problem(s) posed;
- produce a written or oral report setting out solutions and making recommendations.

It is fair to say that case studies tend to be more popular with recruiters working for large organizations. The cases chosen usually focus on a real or imaginary problem, which is used to generate a wide range of individual and group activities. For further guidance see **Chapter 7**.

## Presentations

Increasingly, employers across all occupational sectors are seeking to recruit employees with good oral communication skills – very few job roles now escape this requirement. Hence, during an assessment centre or multi-assessment event you will be placed in a variety of situations (ie interviews, group discussion and presentations) in which you are required to deploy those skills.

Any number of different approaches can be utilized in presentation exercises. For example, you could be asked to give a short presentation on a given subject. If you are given advance notice of this, you should have a chance to do some preparation, eg a candidate for a postgraduate studentship might be asked to read a journal article and to give a critical review of it in the form of a 15-minute presentation. However, if you are 'thrown in at the deep end' with little or no time to prepare what you want to say and how best to say it, your ability to 'think on your feet' becomes paramount. In other circumstances, you might be asked to analyse some case study material, eg data relating to a particular problem, and to use that as the basis for your presentation, which might take the form of a proposed solution to the problem. Clearly, the presentation will provide the assessors with evidence of your knowledge and understanding of the topic under consideration as well as your ability to:

- think logically in order to structure the content of your presentation;

- deploy information in such a way as to make a case or advance an argument;
- speak clearly and audibly to an audience;
- use language (including technical terminology or 'jargon') appropriately;
- use PowerPoint with confidence and skill;
- handle stress, deal with your emotions and appear composed and self-confident under pressure.

To sum up, you must expect your oral communication skills (including your ability to give an effective presentation) to come under close scrutiny at an assessment centre or as part of a multi-assessment event. The means by which this is done, and the contexts in which it occurs, can vary between assessment events. Nevertheless, you should be prepared for it to happen at some stage – perhaps within the framework of a wider assessment exercise such as a case study. More detailed guidance is given in **Chapter 3**.

## In-tray/in-box exercises

With these exercises, candidates are usually asked to adopt a particular role as an employee in a fictitious organization and to deal with the contents of an imaginary in-tray or in-box. Typically, this consists of a sample of internal memos, letters, e-mails, faxes, phone messages and reports. These items will have been chosen to ensure that they vary in their importance, complexity and urgency. The precise details of the task will vary from one assessment centre or event to another, but you will probably be asked to respond in writing to each item and to make a note of the reasons behind your chosen course of action in every case. Such exercises are often given a greater sense of reality by the inclusion of a developing crisis or problem, which you will be expected to resolve whilst dealing with the other items in the in-tray. To add to the pressure, new items may be introduced at any time during the exercise – perhaps in the form of an email arriving in an in-box, or an urgent fax message.

From your performance on the in-tray exercises, the assessors will expect to gather evidence of your ability to:

- analyse and solve problems;
- organize and prioritize tasks whilst under pressure;
- delegate tasks to others as and when it is appropriate to do so;
- manage your time efficiently;
- read quickly with understanding;
- write effectively for particular audiences.

In-tray/in-box exercises are essentially an attempt to simulate the conditions you might expect to encounter in real workplaces, in order to observe how well you can cope with the contingencies that typically occur within them. As such the exercises will be expected to provide the assessors with a wide range of first-hand evidence about you, and since these exercises are rapidly becoming the norm, make sure that your IT skills are well developed before you attend an assessment centre. Assessors, whilst implicitly assessing these skills, will not be expecting to find flaws in what by now should be a set of high-level competencies. More detailed guidance is given in **Chapter 7**.

## Assessing your performance

The important thing to remember about how you will be assessed at an assessment centre is that a variety of methods will be used to gather information about you. Hence, there is no single way in which your performance will be judged. For example, the method used to mark your answers in an ability test will be very different from that used to assess your performance on a group discussion exercise. After you have taken the test, your test paper will be marked objectively – in all probability electronically – to produce a total score. The assessors will already have predetermined what the minimum score (or 'pass mark') should be for that particular selection exercise. They may have decided, for example, that a high score has to be achieved on one of the tests because it will provide an accurate measure of your ability in an area of competence (eg numeracy) considered to be essential for the appointment they are seeking to make. Indeed, in some cases, it may not be possible for candidates to compensate for a low mark on that one component by their performance on the other exercises.

By comparison, the observation methods used to assess your performance on many of the other exercises will appear to be more subjective. However, particular care will have been taken to make sure that the assessors' collective judgements are both valid and reliable. Validity is achieved by basing judgements on assessment criteria derived from a careful analysis of the requirements of the job, training opportunity or education programme under consideration. The use of agreed criteria increases the reliability of assessment by ensuring that the assessors are all looking for the same things and evaluate their worth in the same way. From time to time assessors will cross-check their judgements in order to eliminate, or at least minimize, variations in assessment from one assessor to another.

You will always be able to recognize the assessors – they will usually be the ones making notes. This is because the score each candidate achieves on an assessment activity is being carefully recorded on a master sheet, in order to build up profiles of candidates' strengths and weaknesses. Ultimately, this information will be used in the deliberations that lead to the final selection(s) being made.

## Social activities and events

If you take another look at the sample timetables given in **Figure 1.2** and **Figure 1.3** it will not escape your notice that, in addition to the time that is devoted to tests and assessment exercises, candidates are usually expected to participate in some form of social activity or event. This may well consist of no more than a buffet lunch at which you will have an opportunity to meet and talk informally to other people – fellow candidates, recent entrants to the organization, former students, managers and assessors. Time may also have been set aside for a site visit and meetings with representatives from the organization other than those involved in the assessment process. You should bear in mind that these are not just 'time-fillers' – they will have been structured into the programme deliberately and they are there to serve specific purposes. As such they will give you an opportunity to relax and unwind a little, and to ask those questions that are important to you, eg about the job, the organization and the wider context in which the organization functions, including its operating environment. It is worth giving prior thought, therefore, to what those questions might be – and in so doing remember that different people might well give you different answers to the same question.

There is only one rule. Don't be lulled into thinking that social time and the related activities are so unimportant that you can afford just to relax and 'let your hair down'. Indeed, someone could be waiting to catch you 'off your guard' before asking you a really searching question. Hence, you would be well advised on occasions such as these to show that you are socially aware and sensitive to the needs of the situation by:

- being willing to mix socially with those who are present, and to engage with them in polite conversation;

- communicating through your actions (including your body language) that you are interested and alert, eg by listening and responding to what others are saying;
- being polite, courteous and sociable to everyone you meet irrespective of their status;
- if alcohol is on offer, controlling your intake and making sure that you do not allow yourself to become too relaxed and informal with those present, including the other candidates.

To sum up, there will be opportunities at the assessment centre to socialize – over coffee, at mealtimes and during breaks. You should remember that these provide the assessors with a chance to see how well you can mix with others in commonplace situations. At the same time they give you an opportunity to find out more about the job and the organization and to show that you are socially aware and adept.

## Dress code

Be warned – there are still people around who say things like 'The first points I look for are a good handshake and clean shoes. For me, a limp handshake is an immediate negative. Too much scent bothers me too.' So, you had better firm up those handshakes, polish those shoes and have someone you trust check out your scent. Having done that, you need to avoid fidgeting and remember to make eye contact with the people to whom you are introduced – including the interviewers. Seriously, first impressions do count. Put yourself in the interviewers' or assessors' shoes (hopefully clean) – what would you like to see and hear when you first meet a candidate?

What you choose to wear might well be a matter that is largely taken out of your hands if you are asked to adhere to a certain 'dress code' at the assessment centre. The term to watch out for here is 'smart casual'. Experience suggests that some people are likely to err on the 'smart' side of the injunction, whereas others (from experience mostly men, we suggest) have a tendency to seize on the 'casual' at the expense of the 'smart'. Probably, the safest course of action is to wear a suit – after all you can easily shed the jacket or undo the buttons so that the 'smart' can quickly become 'casual' and vice versa.

Some of the key points about dress to bear in mind are:

- If you have any doubts about the dress code, check it out in advance – it only requires a telephone call and no one will think ill of you for enquiring.
- Make certain you and your clothes are clean, smart and tidy – the interviewers will see this as a reflection of you and your attitudes.
- Don't wear overbearing perfume or aftershave – you don't want the interviewers to remember you as the one who gave them a headache.
- Make sure you are comfortable with what you wear – you will be less self-conscious and more self-confident if you are.
- Your appearance should show others how you think and feel about yourself – so be positive.

## Punctuality

Punctuality is a simple matter – it's about getting where you have to be on time every time. So, it's in your best interest to make sure that you arrive at the venue at the appointed hour, not least because if you are late you may well be excluded from participating in the proceedings. Once you have arrived at the location, getting to where you need to be on time should not be a problem. However, arriving late for one of the activities (eg an interview or a group exercise) does happen, and when it does it can be a great source of irritation – not least because (as we have stressed) assessment events are always run to a very tight schedule. So, make sure that you are always punctual. You can do this by knowing where you have to be and for what purpose, and the time you have to be there. Remember, if you are late just once, your aberration might appear to have gone unnoticed; do it more than once and it certainly will not!

## Advance preparation

It would be easy to adopt the attitude that you can't prepare for an assessment centre, as you can for an examination, or that it is better just to 'trust to luck'. Nothing could be further from the truth, as the contents of this book demonstrate. So here is a checklist of ideas that will help you to prepare for, and do your best at, an assessment centre or multi-assessment event:

- Dispel the idea that you cannot prepare in advance – there are many sensible things you can do to improve your chances of success if you are willing to make the effort.
- If you have had some previous experience with ability tests and personality inventories it will be to your advantage. As you will find out in **Chapter 4** and **Chapter 5** there are plenty of books and websites that feature practice tests and inventories you can use.
- Put your back into preparation and really mean it – don't just go through the motions.
- If you are given any preparatory information or materials, make certain that you read them carefully in advance – they were given to you for a good reason.
- Take another look at any information you were given in advance, eg the job description or anything about the organization, to see if it gives any clues as to the type of person the organization is seeking or the questions you might be asked in an interview.

- If you know people who work in the organization, or one similar to it, check out what they have to say – but don't allow yourself to be unduly influenced by their experiences.
- Check out what is available on assessment centres via the internet – various organizations, including universities, provide useful information on their websites on what to expect (steers are given later).
- Talk to friends and acquaintances about what you can learn from their experiences of attending an assessment centre/multi-assessment event.
- Try to ensure that you arrive at the venue feeling as relaxed and well rested as you can – it can be a very exacting and tiring experience and you will need to have all your wits about you.
- Try to be yourself by acting as naturally as you can. In other words, don't try to manipulate the impression that you give, because you won't be able to sustain it.
- Review your experience to date (eg, as a student or in previous employment) in order to identify what you have learned which is relevant to the job, training opportunity or education course for which you have applied.
- Once you are at the centre, if you think that you have not performed well in a particular assessment, try not to let this adversely affect your performance on the other exercises. You might not have done as badly as you think and it may well be that your overall performance will be more important.
- Consider the interactions at the assessment centre to be a two-way process – for the recruiters to discover what they want to know about you, and for you to find out more about the organization and the job or the training opportunity, or the course for which you have applied.
- Try to think of the assessment event not just as a means of getting a job or a place on a training programme, but also as

an opportunity to partake of a positive learning experience from which you can only benefit.

That is a lot to be getting on with but it is not really so much if you are absolutely set on landing that job or that place on a course. Firstly, work your way through this book, following the advice and guidance provided in the individual chapters, then undertake an audit of your personal skills using the framework provided in the **Appendix**. This two-stage approach is strongly advised.

2

# *How to succeed in group exercises*

The **aim** of this chapter is to familiarize you with the different types of group exercises in which you might be asked to participate at an assessment centre or as part of a multi-assessment event. These include activities that range from short 'icebreaker' exercises to longer activities involving group discussion. The chapter also provides you with guidance on such matters as: how to contribute to group processes; completing tasks; knowing when and how to negotiate and/or compromise; and the assessment criteria used by assessors. Above all, the aim is to help you prepare for the group exercises you are likely to encounter.

## Group exercises in the assessment process

Group exercises provide evidence which is difficult to obtain by other means. For example, these exercises enable the assessors to observe people interacting with each other, and displaying behaviours such as interrupting other group members or remaining silent when they could be contributing to the discussion – traits which might otherwise have gone unnoticed. In terms of their cost effectiveness, group exercises provide recruiters with much valuable evidence in a relatively short period of time – evidence that can be augmented with the data obtained by other methods of assessment, thereby providing a richer mix of information about the candidates than would otherwise be possible.

Critics of group exercises are apt to say that they reward those candidates who possess what is known colloquially as the 'gift of the gab'. However, this is not the case, because having such a 'gift' is not necessarily an advantage, especially if the talk consists of no more than empty platitudes. Experienced assessors rarely reward such behaviour. That said, you should never be afraid of making lengthy contributions to the discussion because you think the assessors might view them unfavourably. After all, the whole point of the exercises is that the assessors want to be able to hear what you have to say, and how you say it, in the context of the group's interchanges. So, once you 'have the floor', the best thing you can do is to speak easily and to the point, taking care to carry the discussion forward. If, as happens all too often, someone is trying to monopolize the discussion, it is up to you, working in conjunction with others in the group, to 'persuade' that person to stop talking and listen to what the others have to say. In so doing, remember that it will be in your best interests to act courteously but firmly. The assessors will take note of such behaviour and reward you accordingly.

While they can never entirely replicate the 'true to life' situations that occur in the workplace, group exercises have enough points in their favour to justify their inclusion in the programme of an assessment centre or multi-assessment event. Firstly, they are fair to all candidates because they give everyone the same opportunity, under the same conditions, to show how effectively they can function as a member of a working group. Secondly, because they do not usually require any particular specialist knowledge, people from diverse backgrounds and with different experiences can contribute with equal effectiveness providing that the standard of their spoken English is adequate for the purpose. Language competence is clearly an important issue in exercises where oral interaction is at the heart of the activity, but in making their judgements the assessors will endeavour to take individual variations into account in order to ensure that all candidates are treated fairly and equally.

So what must you do in order to perform to the best of your ability in assessment exercises that involve working in a group? Experience suggests that you need to bear in mind the following points:

- Be yourself at all times, ie do not try to project a 'different' image as you will find it difficult to sustain and it will do you no good in the long run.
- Don't talk just for the sake of talking. The quality of what you say is likely to be more important than the quantity.
- Listen carefully to what other members of the group have to say – but in so doing don't lapse into silence.
- There is nothing virtuous about saying nothing. By keeping quiet you are missing an opportunity to demonstrate what may be your greatest strengths – so try to make as many positive contributions to the discussion as circumstances permit.
- Remember that people with very different styles can perform with equal effectiveness – it is not a competition to see who can dominate the interactions of the group.

## What the assessors are looking for

Although you may not like it, you simply have to accept the presence of the assessors in the room. However unobtrusive they try to be, you will be conscious of their presence. In particular, you will notice that one of them is sitting opposite you, maybe not directly opposite, but opposite enough for you to recognize that this is your assessor. Having registered that fact, the best thing you can do is to forget about him or her. Above all, do not try to: establish eye contact with the assessor; address your remarks to the assessor; look at the assessor when someone says something with which you disagree; or make a fuss if and when the interactions in the group 'take a turn for the worse'. Such behaviour will only signal to the assessor that you are 'putting on a show' for his or her benefit, or that you lack confidence in what you are saying – none of which will be to your advantage.

In observing your behaviour in the group exercises, the assessors will be asking the following questions:

- Are you able to help the group achieve its objectives, eg by identifying ways of tackling the problem?
- Can you 'think on your feet', eg by responding to a suggestion made by another member of the group?
- Can you speak effectively in front of others, eg by expressing your views clearly and making yourself heard by the rest of the group?
- Can you inject some structure into the discussion, eg by helping the group to organize its ideas and to frame a coherent response?
- Can you build on what others say, eg in order to broaden the discussion or the collective analysis of the problem?
- Can you help to get the best out of the group, eg by drawing others into the discussion or by challenging those who are wasting the group's time on irrelevancies?
- Can you help to drive the group forward, eg by suggesting ways of completing the task in hand?

In making their judgements, the assessors will also be looking for evidence that you possess, or have the potential to develop, competence in the following areas:

- interpersonal or 'people' skills, including your ability to empathize with others;
- leadership skills, including your ability to influence other people;
- communication skills – both verbal and non-verbal;
- focus on results, including your goal-orientation, motivation and achievement drive;
- working with others, including your teamwork skills.

However strong you think you are in relation to each of these areas of competence, we suggest that you find the time needed to complete the self-audits provided in the **Appendix** at the end of this book. The results should help you to build up a profile of the strengths on which you can build, and the weaknesses you will need to address if you are to do justice to yourself at an assessment centre/multi-assessment event.

When evaluating performance in the group exercises, the chances are that your assessors will be working to a set of agreed assessment criteria in the form of performance indicators. The ones given in **Figure 2.1** for 'teamwork' are intended to give you an idea of what these indicators might look like, though in practice there would be a few more. Notice that each indicator A to E is given a mark between 1 and 7 (only 1 and 7 are shown here) before an overall score is determined. This is not necessarily an arithmetical average – it can be arrived at by reviewing the overall distribution of scores.

Of course, you do not have to be an over-enthusiastic team player, or pretend to be one – recruiters do not expect that in everyone, or even in most of the people they select. However, if they have gone to the trouble of identifying teamwork as a desirable area of competence, the least they can expect is that you recognize the importance of the 'team ethic' – and in so doing that you are willing to suppress your ego in the wider interests of the group. In short, what they will be looking for is evidence of your ability to work effectively with others.

| | | |
|---|---|---|
| A | Treats people with courtesy and respect at all times | 7 |
| | Shows no courtesy or respect | 1 |
| B | Shows interest in what others have to say | 7 |
| | Shows no interest in what others have to say | 1 |
| C | Contributes ideas freely and openly | 7 |
| | Keeps ideas, if any, to herself/himself | 1 |
| D | Offers non-verbal support to others | 7 |
| | Withholds non-verbal support to others | 1 |
| E | Tries to understand where others are coming from | 7 |
| | Makes no effort to understand where others are coming from | 1 |

**Key points of performance:**
What was done well?
What could have been done better?

**Overall rating 7 6 5 4 3 2 1**

**Figure 2.1** Performance indicators used in assessing teamwork in a group exercise

Once in a group, individuals who are determined to pursue their own agendas are easy to identify. When people preface interventions with 'From my point of view…' or 'It seems to me that…' or 'As I said before…', you can be sure that they are thinking of themselves and not about the group and its common tasks. Be aware that, if you persist in repeating a point from a personal perspective over and over again, the assessors will simply write something like 'self-centred and repetitive' in their notes.

Organizations do not expect all or even most of the candidates invited to attend an assessment centre to be driven, 'can-do' obsessives. What they are looking for, via the assessors, are people who are capable of tackling a problem in conjunction with others, when working within strict time constraints. As for those constraints, it is not uncommon to hear candidates muttering among themselves such sentiments as 'It wouldn't be like that in real life – we would have far longer to do that'.

Experience tells us that assessors will routinely ignore utterances of this kind – and may even deduct marks from the culprits' overall scores for the exercise. So, even if you think the task you have been set is unrealistic, keep your thoughts to yourself. Take the task at face value and do your best to solve the problem by working as hard and constructively as you can with the others in your group.

## Assigned, non-assigned and assumed roles

Basically, three types of group discussion exercise are used at assessment centres:

- **Assigned roles**, in which not all of the candidates are given the same working brief, ie some of its elements will be common to all, and some will be assigned to individuals.
- **Non-assigned roles**, in which all members of the group are given the same brief.
- **Assumed roles**, in which there is no working brief provided, ie people assume roles by virtue of previous work experiences that they take into the exercise. Typically, this is based on the discussion of an issue that has been the subject of a presentation.

### Assigned roles

The advantages of group exercises based on having assigned roles are that they:

- lend themselves to more realistic scenarios;
- allow better assessment of some areas of competence like investigative and negotiating skills;
- give everyone an equal opportunity to contribute to the group's interactions and decision making.

It follows that having assigned roles means that no one has any excuse for not contributing to the proceedings. This makes it easier for the assessors to recognize underperformance on the part of an individual candidate. The disadvantage of assigned roles exercises from a candidate's point of view is that you may be allocated a role with which you feel uncomfortable. If so, just accept it as part of the challenge – the chances are that others in your group will feel the same.

The smartest way to treat an assigned role – whether you like the role or not – is to try to do justice to yourself in that role. The trick is not to allow yourself to be too constrained by the way the role has been defined. So, once you have succeeded in negotiating what you would regard as the sticking points of your brief, or have given way gracefully under superior reasoning and persuasion, you should work towards achieving the best solution to the problem from the organization's point of view. After all, in real-life situations no one would be expected to go on arguing about too narrow a functional brief or role definition.

## Non-assigned roles

The advantage of group exercises with non-assigned roles is that they allow leaders to emerge – the same applies to group exercises with assumed roles. Remember, however, that there is no reason why leadership should not be exercised in a group exercise in which the roles have been assigned.

## Assumed roles

If you are asked to start by giving a five-minute presentation, which is then followed by open discussion once everybody has given their presentation, you are being asked to take on an assumed role. Your role is to argue your case based on what you have said in your presentation, whilst being prepared to concede or lend your support to an alternative argument or solution if that is justified by what has been said in the discussion. In that sense, you are simply playing yourself and as such you are not constrained by an artificial or unwanted brief. That said, you still have to make sense of issues that might be alien to you and come up with some sensible things to say, especially in your presentation.

## Tactical considerations

With group work exercises you should be aware of certain tactical considerations. These are related to group dynamics – the positions people may come to occupy in the group and the inner motivation that drives their actions. In these situations there are usually two major positions, and one of minor importance. The major positions are chair and scribe. The other role is that of timekeeper – a job that can usually be done by the chair or the scribe as part of his or her wider role.

It would be easy to think that being the chair or scribe (especially the former) will give you an advantage – not least because it will give you an opportunity to lead the discussion and in so doing gain the attention of the assessors. Sometimes groups believe so strongly in the advantages conferred on the person who becomes the chair (though without vocalizing it to each other) that they refuse to appoint one, usually with dire consequences. The role of the scribe is not usually seen as being so advantageous, because of the nature of the work it involves. However, if you do take it on, be aware that it may put you in a position to influence the decisions made by the group, if not lead the interactions. Consequently, it is worth taking a look in more detail at the three positions.

## Chair

If you are tempted by the prospect of being the chair, make sure that you are able to do the job before you volunteer or allow yourself to be nominated. Assuming the role of chair carries with it a tariff: do it well and you can benefit in how you are assessed; do it badly and your score may well suffer by comparison with others in the group, notably with the person who manages to salvage something from the wreckage you have created. The best advice, therefore, is to be wary of anyone who tries to flatter you into taking on the job – 'You look as if you know what you are doing, so you be chair.' If you don't take care, before you know where you are you will find yourself managing (or trying to manage) the interactions of the group. There is really no need to allow yourself to get caught out in these circumstances. After all, the chances are that you will hardly know the people with whom you have been asked to work, so why respond to their flattery, especially if it is not in your best interests to do so?

In group discussion exercises a good chair manages the interactions, making sure above all that everyone is brought into the discussion and then facilitating the process by making timely interventions, curtailing rambling contributions and generally moving things along towards the achievement of an agreed outcome. The chair does not have to do all of those things because some room must be left for others to demonstrate that they too are capable of taking appropriate action. However, in essence that is the job description. If you do not feel confident about carrying out responsibilities such as these, then don't volunteer and don't allow yourself to be pressured into accepting someone else's nomination. An assessment centre or a multi-assessment event is not the place to experiment if in so doing all you are likely to do is to fall short of the expected standard.

Experience indicates that it is much better to have a chair in a group discussion exercise than to try to proceed without one. After all, if the person you select turns out to be incompetent, then the group can tacitly drop the person, and you are all no worse off than you were before. Observation of chairless groups shows that they are usually rambling, directionless and low on creative energy. So, unless the people in a group know what they are doing, and the chances are that a group like the one you will be involved in at an assessment centre will not, the advice is to cooperate fully with your fellow group members in the selection of a chair.

Wilfully not nominating a chair is really a defensive ploy designed to ensure that no one benefits too much from the exercise – better we all score 4/10 than for someone to score 8/10, the reasoning seems to go. It is, however, a line of thinking that could be very dangerous. For example, unbeknown to you the assessors could be operating a 'hurdles' system whereby, to be successful, candidates are required to reach a minimum score on every exercise. Hence, you could be damaging your own chances of success at the outset of the exercise by colluding with the rest of the group in making such a decision.

## Scribe

There is a poisoned chalice element to being the designated scribe, but then there are risks attached to refusing the job if it is offered to you or failing to volunteer your services. With scribe, the secret of success is to serve the interests of the group by making a solid contribution, but not to spend too much time simply writing down what other people have said. Again, be careful not to allow yourself to be lured into the job. Given that there are always people who will say 'My handwriting is hopeless' or words to that effect, you might, if you believe your handwriting is better than that, react by putting up your hand to volunteer your services. However, there is usually no shortage of people waiting to take on the role. People do this because they think it will give them visibility and with it the chance to shape the group's outcome. They are right to think like this – but it is a long way between thought and execution. Just as with the chair, you have to know what you are doing, and you need to know when to stop writing – keeping strictly to the role all the way through a group discussion exercise is not a good idea.

Just as with chair, if you want to be scribe you had better be confident that you are able to do the job well. To be an effective scribe you actually do need to have good, clear handwriting, but that is only for starters. What really matters is your ability to structure and organize the outcomes of the group's deliberations so that anyone could go to the flipchart after the group has left and the contents of what you have written would make sense. Experience suggests that the ability to do this is far from common. So if you become the scribe make sure: that the group helps you to formulate a structure for your note taking; and that you use it from the start. Remember, the worst thing that you can do as the scribe is to try to write down everything the group offers, as this is likely to come without any prior processing. If you do that, all that you will have to show for your efforts will be an incoherent list of ideas and suggestions.

The next hazard is to avoid becoming too attached to your creation. It is all too easy to stop, admire and tinker with what you have written on the flipchart, oblivious to what the rest of the group is saying. A worse trap to fall into is to add material of your own devising. Anyone who does this has clearly forgotten that his or her primary role is to capture and express the thoughts and suggestions emanating from the group – not to write up his or her own version of how the set task or problem should be resolved.

So, why should you avoid becoming too attached to being the scribe? It is not a matter of 'overstaying your welcome' – the group will probably be quite happy for you to continue. Should you put the pen down, the chances are that someone will hand it back to you to indicate that you should keep going. Ignore such overtures – if you think about it, standing down is in *your* own interests. Think about it for a moment. In a fast-moving discussion, what is the most difficult to do given that you are meant to listen closely to what is being said, think how best it can be expressed *and* write it down within the agreed structure? Obviously, the most difficult thing to do is making meaningful contributions to the discussion. Some people are fortunate enough to be able to do all those tasks at the same time, but it is extremely difficult to do all of them well. So, it is far better to do a period of duty as the scribe and then to stand down gracefully, taking care to find a form of words more persuasive than 'Could someone else take over now?' Someone should be ready and willing to do so – after all, if scribes are expected to contribute to the discussion then members of the group should be ready to take on the role.

Sometimes groups jump too readily into appointing a scribe, as if it were a safety blanket. The danger, as with chair and timekeeper, is that if you get someone else to do the work you don't have to do it yourself – you can forget about it. You don't categorically need a scribe. What is wrong with members of the group taking their own notes and then, when the time is right, collectively converting them into a summary? In such circumstances a scribe becomes superfluous.

## Timekeeper

Having someone keep the time is necessary, but insufficient to make sure the group completes its deliberations in good time. It is all very well someone shouting out the time, but if the group is failing to make headway with its common task there seems little point – far better to call out the time and make some positive suggestions as to how things could be moved forward. If you like, it is the timekeeper acting as group 'enforcer' – but isn't that a job for the chairperson? In reality, everyone in the group should be their own timekeeper – it is not too difficult to keep track of the time especially if there is a clock in the room, as there usually is.

So, do not expect to pick up many credits from the assessors by being the timekeeper – unless, as indicated above, you do something else in addition to calling out the time. Also, if you are going to be the timekeeper, make sure that you get it right! Amazing as it may sound, it is not unknown for the designated timekeeper to call out the wrong time and in so doing seriously mislead the group.

## Icebreaker exercises

'Icebreakers' are exercises that are intended to get the proceedings at an assessment centre under way by encouraging the participants to interact with each other. They are based on the supposition that everyone present is likely to be nervous and a bit 'on edge' and needs a 'warm-up' activity to help break down inhibitions – to 'unfreeze'. Such icebreaker exercises can vary from the perfunctory to the more elaborate.

An example of the former is a widely used icebreaker, which simply involves going round the table asking people in turn to tell the rest of the group who they are. The next step would then be for everyone to tell the group three things about themselves, which no one sitting at the table would be expected to know, including an unfulfilled ambition. There is obviously an opportunity here for humour and even boasting, which the extroverts will usually grasp. But generally it is harmless fun, and it does not really matter if you don't believe that someone wants to row across the Atlantic in a bathtub. The main thing is that it gets people talking and stirs the adrenalin, which is the purpose of the exercise. Notice that this is not strictly a group exercise, but an individual activity done with a group acting as the audience.

Where the activities at an assessment centre are based on a running scenario involving a fictitious organization you may find that an icebreaker exercise is used to help you get inside that organization. Thus if the organization is called 'As You Like It Leisure' and you have applied for a real job in the marketing department, you may well be given a background document containing relevant information and asked to explore it with one or more of the other members of the group. For such a task where people work in pairs, the instructions might well be like those given in **Figure 2.2**.

Icebreaker exercises, like the one described in **Figure 2.2**, pose a gentle challenge to the participants, but since they will always be non-assessed you have nothing to fear. Use them as an opportunity to acclimatize yourself to the atmosphere of the assessment centre/multi-assessment event, and to prepare yourself for the sterner tests that will inevitably follow.

## Professional role-players

Group exercises can involve some form of role-play other than that involved in following an assigned brief. It is becoming quite commonplace for professional role-players or actors to be

This is a non-assessed exercise designed to give you the opportunity to become familiar with the fictitious organization around which the assessment centre exercises have been designed.

Information about this organization is contained in the attached brief entitled: 'As You Like It Leisure: the assessment centre scenario'.

You will work in pairs. Your task is to read the brief and then animate the As You Like It Leisure organization and its past and current changes in a visual format that can be presented to the rest of the group within a five-minute time slot.

(There then follows an outline – which is not provided here – of the company and the particular challenges and specific issues it is facing, especially in the Marketing Department.)

**Figure 2.2** An example of an icebreaker exercise

introduced into group exercises, usually after the discussion has commenced. The purpose of this is to provide a focus and context for the group's activities before the professional role-players arrive. Once they are there, they can be briefed to influence the group's behaviour, eg by requesting to see its plans, or asking for clarification of its aims and objectives. They can also be instructed to disagree with the group to see how adept its members are at defusing conflicts of opinion and moving the discussion forward.

If you find yourself in this situation, do not make the mistake of treating the professional role-players as an amusing sideshow. Their deliberate intrusion into the exercise has a serious part to play in the assessment process. The purpose is to enhance the quality of the interaction by introducing an appropriate element of realism into the proceedings. In so doing, the intervention of professional role-players ensures that the evidence on which assessment decisions will be based is thrown into sharper relief than would otherwise have been the case. So, do not make the mistake of taking it all too lightly. Candidates have been observed to be amused when professional role-players squabble or appear to overreact – and even look at the assessors in disbelief! Your interests will be better served by concentrating your attention on the task in hand by trying to show how well you are able to cope with the authentic, 'real-life' situation that the professional role-players have created.

Even though they may have been informed that the professional role-players will arrive at a designated time, it is not uncommon for groups to be ill prepared for their arrival. How often have we seen groups still crowded round the flipchart thrashing out the details of what to do while the actors, having entered the room without being noticed, have to wait before their presence is acknowledged? Nothing is more certain to get your group off on the wrong foot – especially if the actors begin to behave like angry customers or clients.

## Preparing for group discussion exercises

The chances are that you will find it difficult to persuade your friends, relatives or colleagues to join you in a mock discussion, and even if you did it could prove to be counter-productive because for them there will be nothing at stake. So, the best course of action for you is to focus on specific skills, and how and when you might be required to demonstrate your ability to use them. The self-audits provided in the **Appendix** are intended to help you in this respect. In particular you would be well advised to look carefully at 'Oral communication skills' and 'Working with others'. This should prompt you to ask yourself how well you speak in front of others, and whether or not you are able to conquer your nerves. The advice is to be positive and think of times when you managed to do it successfully without hesitation or finding it difficult to think of anything relevant to say.

Similarly, you should ask yourself what sort of team player you really are. In this respect it is vital that you develop a realistic understanding of yourself. This is because many people, without thinking about it too much, imagine that they are good at working with others in a team. Unfortunately, the truth can often be something else. For example, one of the authors of this book knows that he is not really a team player. However, he also knows that he is not an out-and-out individualist, which means that he can work within a team for particular purposes and for certain periods of time.

Group exercises tend to attract a certain amount of apprehension – even animosity – on the part of candidates. They are widely regarded as something to be endured – as a means to an end. Our advice is not to be drawn into this line of thinking. Instead, we suggest that you try to be the one person at the assessment centre who takes the group discussion exercise seriously, and who shows some enthusiasm for it. When you see the activity coming up on the programme, get your mind in focus and tell yourself that this is an assessment exercise on which you can score highly relative to the other candidates.

## What assessors do *not* want to see

There are certain behaviours that assessors do not want to see during group discussion exercises – or to be more correct, they don't mind seeing it because it gives them strong evidence on which to base their judgements. Here are some things to avoid doing:

- Negative non-verbal behaviour such as sitting apart from the rest of the group, turning your back on the others or looking petulant as if you would rather leave and 'take your ball home' with you.
- Talking while someone else has the floor, interrupting others when they are in full flow, or acting in a manner that might be construed as verbal aggression or bullying.
- Taking a unilateral decision to allocate jobs (such as scribe, chair and timekeeper) to other people in the group.
- Showing that you have not mastered the brief by constantly poring over the paperwork.
- Ridiculing what someone else has to say.
- Wasting the group's time because you have misinterpreted the information or misunderstood what someone has said.
- Keeping quiet while at the same time managing to look disinterested and 'above it all'.
- Cracking jokes – especially those to which some members of the group might well take exception.

Commit too many of these 'misdemeanours' and it is likely that the assessors will draw the conclusion that you do not possess the emotional intelligence – especially empathy and social skills

– you need to be able to work effectively in group situations. They may even come to the conclusion that, as a person you lack self-awareness and self-regulation and, as such, someone who might prove to be a disruptive influence in the workplace. However, if you can observe the rules, which really only requires you to exercise a degree of self-control, and manage to engage constructively in the group's work to the extent that you are adding value by your presence, then you will have a good chance of attracting a positive evaluation from the assessors. You might even enjoy this part of the assessment centre experience.

3

# How to make successful presentations

If you attend an assessment centre or even a multi-assessment event you can expect to be asked to give an oral presentation of some kind. It may take the form of an individual or a group presentation. The audience may be one or more assessors only or, more rarely, a mixture of assessors and other candidates. Like others before you, you will probably find the prospect of giving a presentation somewhat daunting – but just remember even experienced presenters often feel like that. However, they know from experience that it is better to be slightly keyed up with their adrenalin flowing than so 'laid-back' that they fail to perform to the best of their ability. The fact is that presentation skills have never been more important in the selection process. The **aim** of this chapter, therefore, is to provide you with guidance on: planning and preparing for a presentation; delivering it effectively; and how your delivery of it will be assessed.

## Planning and preparation

A good starting point, if you have not already done so, would be to undertake an audit of your oral communication skills using the checklist provided in the **Appendix**. If your self-evaluation is a true reflection of your ability, you should learn something about the strengths on which you can build and the areas for improvement you need to address.

With presentations, thorough planning and preparation are essential to success, especially if you are relatively inexperienced. You really can prepare for these events and, in so doing, reap the rewards. If we had to provide just one piece of advice it would be this – get the content right and the delivery should follow suit. That is not to say that it will take care of itself – you will still have lots of work to do. However, if you go into a presentation still unsure about whether you should say this or that, or how to start ('Will that attempt at light-hearted humour backfire?'), or have too much material and are dithering at the last minute about what to use and what to leave out, then your confidence is likely to crumble in front of your audience. Good, well-organized content is the prerequisite for an effective presentation.

So, what should your preparation include? The first thing to do is to make certain that you follow closely any instructions you have been given. In this respect, you should pay particular attention to the following aspects of your brief:

- what you are expected to talk about (ie the subject matter of your presentation);
- the time you have been allocated;
- whether or not you are expected to invite, or to answer, questions from your audience.

You should also be prepared for the possibility that your presentation will be video-recorded – it will enable your performance to be reviewed later by the assessors as part of the assessment selection process. If that turns out to be the case, don't allow yourself to be 'thrown' by the presence of the camera – just try to carry on with your presentation as if it wasn't there. That should not be too difficult because the equipment will probably be in a fixed position at some point in the room and should simply 'blend' into the furniture of the room.

Having established the basic parameters of the exercise you should then try to do what every presenter has to do:

- Find out what your audience is likely to know about the content of your presentation so that you can build upon that knowledge rather than repeating it – though don't make too many assumptions as this can cause problems for you at a later stage.
- Acquire a thorough knowledge of the content of your presentation without overloading your mind with needless information. In so doing, try to separate the important from the unimportant.
- Make any visual aids you plan to use (eg PowerPoint for the overhead projector). If you are creating transparencies, make them as clear as you possibly can, and don't say 'Sorry about the handwriting', because that is not an acceptable excuse.
- Devise an outline plan for the presentation. You may find it helpful to make use of headings, but whatever you do try to restrict yourself to one side of A4 or both sides of a card (see below). There is nothing worse than a speaker having to shuffle around among several pieces of paper.
- Ensure, if possible (it won't always be), that the room in which the presentation is to be delivered is set out correctly for your purposes, that all the equipment you require is present and that you know how to operate it (see the checklist given in **Figure 3.1**). There is a saying, 'Things are

in the saddle', which means just that – inanimate objects are in control. We have all felt the truth of this in practice – so do your level best to make sure that it doesn't happen to you.

## Structuring your presentation

In planning your presentation you should try to break it up into a number of sections, each of which should be given a subtitle or heading. For each section, list the key points you wish to make. You may find it helpful to:

- Write your headings and key points on a wallboard or flipchart in advance.
- If possible, prepare some PowerPoint slides for the purpose – the advantage of this being that you will be able to show each one in turn at the appropriate point in your presentation. Indeed they may help you to keep to the stated content of your presentation.
- Make yourself a set of brief notes on pieces of card (150 × 100 millimetres) – one card per section of your presentation. Cards are much better than paper, so remember to take some with you – you cannot guarantee that they will be available.

The big advantage of using visual aids is that they will be helpful to your audience in marking out the direction you intend to take, thus facilitating concentration and greater understanding. Correct deployment should also ensure that you deal systematically with all the main points in your presentation. Some people manage without visual aids, but you have to have enough confidence to be able to stand in front of the assessors (or sit alongside them) as you deliver your presentation.

## Getting your presentation off to a good start

Try to give a clear and succinct introduction in which you:

- Introduce yourself and, if appropriate, the organization (imaginary or real) that you represent, eg 'My name is... I am currently employed in the Marketing Division of...' We say 'imaginary' because there may be a role-play element built into the brief you have been given.
- Set out the main aims of your presentation. The old advice applies – 'Tell them what you are going to tell them; tell them; then tell them what you have told them.'
- In this regard, indicate how you plan to structure your presentation ('I intend to deal first with the background to the plan, then to explain how that plan will be implemented and to conclude by describing...').
- Tell the audience how you would prefer to deal with questions. If you are prepared to take them at any time, say so. As a token of confidence it will do you no harm in the eyes of the assessors, who may choose to interject to gauge how you deal with their intervention. Be aware though that taking questions at any time can be high-risk in that you can lose your thread or worse unravel. If you would prefer to reserve questions until the end – and this is really preferable unless you are very experienced – you can say something like 'Finally, could I ask you to save your questions until the end of my presentation? However, if I use any technical terms that you don't understand, please feel free to ask me to explain what they mean.' What you have offered here is a sort of 'halfway house', which should not offend anybody.
- Do not under any circumstances apologize for your lack of experience in making presentations. Even if that is the case, what allowances can the assessors possibly make?

## Delivering your presentation

In delivering your presentation you should:

- Use 'marker' words and phrases such as 'The first point I want to make...', 'Secondly...' , 'The most important aspect of company policy has been to...', 'Crucially...', 'Ultimately, it will be up to...' and so forth. What you are doing is to reinforce the structure of your presentation as set out in your introduction.
- Simplify the language used; in particular:
  - Use simple straightforward sentences to avoid confusing the listeners.
  - Make sure that you define any technical terms. Jargon means 'song of the birds' in Greek, but your audience may not understand it.
- Try to exemplify and reinforce what you say by integrating into your presentation examples with which your audience is likely to be familiar. You are succeeding if you manage to:
  - Avoid getting 'bogged down' in detail so that the listeners have too much information to assimilate.
  - Establish and consolidate the main points that you are trying to make.
- Remember to recapitulate or summarize what you have said at predetermined points such as at the end of a section, eg 'The main points, then, of company policy on recruitment and selection are...' Once again, the aim is to help the audience to 'keep track' of where you are in your presentation. If you can remember to do so, this is also a good way for you to keep a check on your timing.

### Keeping your eye on the audience

Make sure to look at the audience while you are talking – establish strong eye contact with them, all of them if they are numerous, especially those at the edges. That is where ex-President Clinton (and for that matter President Obama) is so good as a public speaker. If you watch him closely you will see that he always trains his gaze on the fringes of his audience so as to draw them into his ambit. By doing this he is being inclusive – which is so important when making presentations.

Of course, US presidents usually have the advantage of speaking from an autocue – a luxury you will not be afforded. So, if you do have to keep referring to your notes don't, on any account, bury your head in them. By keeping your head up you can pick up non-verbal clues from the body language of the audience about whether or not they are paying attention to your presentation or are interested in what you are saying. By monitoring the reactions of the audience in that way, you can make some minor changes to what you are saying and how you say it, eg by moving on more quickly than you had intended or pausing to invite a question from the audience. Your rapport with your audience is everything. You can have the most scintillating material (or so you think) but, if your audience isn't onside with you, you are 'dead in the water'. That is why reading their body language is so important.

## Your own body language

Eye contact (or lack of it) is just one form of non-verbal communication used by a speaker during a presentation. Indeed, tone and gesture can be more important than the words you use. You have probably heard it said before: what you say counts for as little as 7 per cent towards the overall impression you make. The figure may not actually be 7 per cent but it is going to be low. So does content matter at all? Of course it does. It is the effort you make with the 7 per cent (what you actually say) that helps you with the other 93 per cent.

With rapport being so crucial to your chances (remember those assessors), you should do your best to create an impression of self-confidence. It starts with standing well – head upright and looking comfortably ahead, chest and shoulders held well, stomach under control and feet slightly apart. Those are the positives; the negatives are: fidgeting with your hands, folding your arms rigidly across your chest (a definite 'no-no') and going on those lengthy 'walkabouts'. Do any of these and you will signal to the audience in no uncertain terms that you are nervous or even defensively under stress. Even what may appear to be a neutral deployment of your arms, by folding them in a 'V' in front of you with one hand over the other, is likely to come across as your being tense. To quell the nerves, a good tip is to hold something in one hand. A card, if you are using one, is a very natural 'prop'. You can also use it to point at a flip sheet or at a transparency. But don't wave it around too much or it will become the focus of the presentation by distracting attention from what you are saying. Alternatively, try to sit well, ie with your upper body as described above, but leaning slightly forward. Be wary, though, of creating a bad impression by slouching casually in the chair. This can happen when you forget where you are and feel the need to be informal or to reduce the tension. What, though, if built into the presentation is an element of role-play that requires you to present to a senior person or board of directors? In these circumstances the last thing you want to appear is casual. Choosing to sit to make your presentation is definitely risky. Because you need to be able to see everybody's face you should only give your presentation from a sitting position when faced with a small audience (eg fewer than 10).

How else can you build rapport with your audience?

- Use gestures (ie movements of the hands and arms) to underline what you are saying. However, avoid movements such as twitches and fidgets and hand chops and spreads that are likely to distract the attention of the audience.

- Use facial expressions (eg smiles, grimaces and expressions of surprise) to reinforce what you are saying – and to make them aware that you are alive.
- Avoid pre-prepared jokes – the best humour is likely to come from unrehearsed comments or ripostes to what other people have said. Even old chestnuts will often bring a smile to the assessors' faces and help release the tension: 'Are you ready to start?' 'As ready as I will ever be.'

## Voice and speech

Try to speak conversationally by imagining that you are talking to people that you know well – the following guidelines should help you to do this:

- Set the 'volume' at the right level at the outset by asking the audience (especially those at the back) if they can all hear you clearly.
- Speak clearly and distinctly.
- Vary the tone of your voice (ie quiet to loud) and the pace of your speech (ie slow to fast).
- Avoid using 'er' and 'um' – it is better to have a silent pause.

## Using visual aids

You may be expected to make use of PowerPoint (or even an overhead projector) as an aid to the delivery of your presentation. If you have had little or no experience of using these, you would be well advised to practise in advance. Take time (you can even ask for it) to become acquainted with how it all works, so that when the time comes for you to start your presentation, you will be free to concentrate on what you are saying and how you are saying it. **Figure 3.1** offers a checklist of dos and don'ts to help you.

**The dos of using visual aids**

✓ Make your projected visual images clear and simple.

✓ Make sure that people in all parts of the room (especially the back) can read them clearly.

✓ Use bullet points rather than large passages of text.

✓ Make sure that their content is consistent with what you are saying.

✓ Make sure they are in the right sequence (ie conform to your plan).

✓ Try to be economic in the number you use – too many diminishes their impact, leads to boredom and can cause you to run out of time.

**The don'ts of using visual aids**

✕ Don't stand in a position that obstructs the audience's view, eg in front of the screen.

✕ Don't talk to the screen instead of the audience – watch how the best TV weather presenters do it.

✕ Don't simply repeat what the audience can read on the screen – it is intended as an aid to what you say, not a substitute.

**Figure 3.1** What to do and what not to do when using visual aids

## Concluding your presentation

Try to bring your presentation to a telling conclusion by:

- letting the audience know that you are coming to the end;
- summarizing the main points you made in your presentation;
- thanking the audience for their attention;
- inviting them to ask questions (if that is part of your brief or part of a 'contract' you made with the audience at the start of your presentation).

## Dealing with questions

Having asked the audience to keep their questions until the end, do not accept them in mid-talk unless you want to. As indicated previously, assessors are often keen to interject. They will usually do this with a specific purpose in mind such as to find out how you respond to an unexpected intervention, ie how well you can think on your feet. However, if you get a really difficult question, from them or some other source, you may find it helpful to:

- Say that you cannot answer it at that moment, but that you will think about it and discuss it with the questioner afterwards.
- Give a tentative or partial answer (in other words, your best current answer) and ask members of the audience if they have anything better to offer.
- Pose a counter-question, eg ask the questioner to explain what lies behind the question. You can even invite the person to suggest an answer – but don't be too cute, as this ploy can backfire if an assessor, seeing what you are trying to do, insists that *you* answer the question.
- Refer questioners to material such as the case study documents in which they can find the answer.

There is nothing wrong with going beyond the question and adding some further thoughts. You may even get credit for doing that – but take care not to overdo it.

# What the assessors will be looking for

The assessors will be looking at, and listening to, your presentation in order to form an overall evaluation of your performance. In so doing they will use a set of assessment criteria and apply a rating scale to each criterion. The precise terms given to these criteria may vary, but in general they will all be looking closely at:

- how well you have planned and prepared your presentation including its content, structure and visual aids;
- the confidence with which you delivered your presentation;
- your oral communication skills, including your style of speaking;
- your skills in using the flipchart, overhead projector or PowerPoint;
- how well you answered questions (ie thought on your feet);
- how well you handled the pressure of the occasion.

## Summary

Much detailed guidance has been provided above on how to succeed in giving presentations. That advice can be summarized as follows:

- Not only is thorough preparation essential, but it will reward you handsomely – never try to give a presentation 'off the cuff'.
- Start with a clear introduction in which you tell the audience what you plan to talk about.
- Give your presentation a clear structure and communicate that to the audience.
- Make a list of key points you intend to make in each section of your address.
- Use marker phrases such as 'The first point I want to make…', 'The most important thing to remember is…' to focus the attention of the audience on what you are saying.
- Use examples purposefully to reinforce and consolidate the points you are making.
- Recap on what you have said at intervals during your presentation.

- Use simple sentences to avoid confusing the listeners.
- Explain any technical terms you use with which your audience might be unfamiliar.
- Take time at the outset to familiarize yourself with the technology.
- Make and maintain eye contact with members of the audience when you are talking to them.
- Carry yourself well throughout – stand up or sit up straight.
- Avoid distracting the audience with unnecessary facial expressions, gestures and hand movements.
- Avoid being overly informal as a way of dealing with the pressure of the situation.
- Conclude by reminding the listeners of the main points that you have made, and inviting questions.

Finally, at the very end of your presentation, don't just grab your notes and bolt for your seat – you will only give the impression that you're glad that the ordeal is over and that you can't wait to get away.

4

# How to excel in psychometric tests

The **aim** of this chapter is to: develop your knowledge and understanding of selection tests; introduce you to different types of psychometric tests; give you opportunities to work through some examples of the most commonly used tests; and offer suggestions on how to prepare for, and pass, such tests. Sources of practice tests are listed in **Further reading from Kogan Page.**

## Tests and why selectors use them

Put simply, tests are designed to measure how good people are at doing certain things – often as a basis for predicting their future performance. Those tests that are designed to measure a person's intellectual capabilities are called 'ability tests', 'cognitive tests' or 'psychometric tests'. Those used at assessment centres or multi-assessment events to select people for jobs, further training or courses of study are usually referred to as 'selection tests'. Such tests seek to establish the extent of the aptitude an applicant has for doing certain kinds of work or for coping with the requirements of particular training opportunities or education courses. The tests used at an assessment centre or multi-assessment event may also include 'personality tests' (sometimes known as 'inventories' or 'questionnaires'), which are designed to measure those aspects of your personality that selectors judge to be relevant to particular jobs or courses. We deal with this form of testing in **Chapter 5**.

In old technology terms, psychometric tests were (and often still are) called 'pencil-and-paper', because that is what you needed to complete them. Now it is customary for tests to be delivered and completed online (see 'Completing psychometric tests online' on page 101). In order to ensure the fairness, consistency and reliability of the results, such tests are:

- taken under standardized conditions including strict adherence to time limits;
- administered by someone who has been trained in their use, and has been certified as competent: in the UK this is done by the British Psychological Society (BPS);
- objectively marked, eg through the use of an electronic scanning machine.

You will find that tests come complete with carefully worded instructions and examples, which tell you exactly what you have to do to complete them correctly. It follows that you need to make a habit on all occasions of reading the test instructions carefully and working through the examples provided even when you think you are already familiar with them. In real tests you will be allowed a set time to do this before the test actually begins, 5 or 10 minutes – so whatever you do don't waste it!

# Types of psychometric test

Recruiters make use of a wide range of tests when selecting candidates. The guidance notes given below are intended to show which areas of competence different tests aim to assess. If you achieve a high score on a particular type of test it may indicate that you will do well in a job or on a training programme or course of study that requires you to apply the skill being tested. On the other hand, if you find that you consistently do badly on a particular test it may be that you would have some difficulty in coping at this stage with jobs or training or study opportunities that require proficiency in the skill being tested. That said, further work on your part to develop that particular skill might enable you to improve your performance on that test at a later date.

**Logical reasoning tests** are used to measure a person's ability to solve problems by thinking logically on the basis of the information provided. These can sometimes take the form of abstract problems, or they can be similar to problems encountered in the kind of work for which people are being selected. The ability to do well on a logical reasoning test may tell you and a potential employer or other selector that you have the ability to think critically and to solve the problems that arise at work or when studying, such as deploying resources, recognizing the limitations of information and data, and forward planning. Some examples from a logical reasoning test are given a little later.

**Numerical reasoning tests** are used to measure the ability to work accurately with numbers and to solve problems based on data presented in various forms such as diagrams, graphs and statistical tables. The ability to do well in this type of test is relevant to situations in which you will be required to work with money, interpret sales or production figures, or cope with the numerical aspects of science and technology. Examples from a variety of numerical reasoning tests are given below.

**Verbal reasoning tests** are used to measure the ability to use language and to comprehend the written word. At work or in study this ability is relevant to tasks such as those that involve reading and writing instructions, letters and reports. At a simple level they may set out to test your basic literacy, including your ability to write grammatically correct sentences and to spell and punctuate correctly. Missing word tests, examples of which are given below, fall into this category. Essentially, verbal reasoning tests are looking for the ability of candidates to understand the meaning of what has been written or said. This capacity to make sense from text is what is being tested in the hidden sentences and sentence sequences test, examples of which are given below.

**Situational judgement tests** are used to assess a person's ability to consistently make the best decisions in difficult circumstances. There are many situations which arise in the workplace where individuals have to review the available information, consider a range of alternative courses of action and then make a decision – usually under the pressure of severe time constraints. Of course many of the other activities used at an assessment centre (eg group, in-tray/in-box and role-play exercises) seek to provide evidence of this ability, but some employers may also ask you to take a specially designed test of situational judgement. Such tests usually consist of a series of scenarios, each of which provides information about an authentic problem placed in context. In each case, the candidate has to read the information, and then make a choice from a range of alternatives. Some examples from a situational judgement test are given later in the chapter.

**Technical tests** are used to measure skills and abilities that are relevant to various kinds of employment. We are talking about tests to assess the ability to understand technical ideas expressed in a mathematical form (including diagrams) or how mechanical things work.

**Clerical tests**, as the name suggests, are used to measure clerical skills such as the facility to check and classify data under time pressure. However, because tests of this type are specific to certain kinds of work, and because these are clerical in nature, it is unlikely that you will encounter them at an assessment centre or a multi-assessment event. Consequently, there are no examples or sample questions in this chapter.

The worked examples and sample questions you are going to meet soon are taken from some of the types of test most commonly used at assessment centres. Work your way through them and you should have a good idea of what is involved in each case. The **answers** to the sample questions are given at the end of the chapter. Working through the sample questions should also help you to begin to identify where your strengths and weaknesses might lie when it comes to taking real tests. However you stand in this regard, you would be well advised to develop your skills further by means of practice tests (see **Further reading from Kogan Page**).

## Examples from a logical reasoning test

Now consider the two sample questions given below. Your task is to work out which is the correct answer in each case, using the information provided. You should:

- Study the data very carefully before you attempt to answer the questions.
- Record your answer by putting a tick (✓) alongside the option(s) you have chosen.
- Use scrap paper for any rough work you need to do.
- Allow yourself about **five minutes** per item – this will help to give you an idea of the time pressure you would have to work under in a real test.

## Question 1

Imagine that you work for a company that offers coach tours of London to visiting tourists. Each coach tour has a courier who gives a commentary for the tourists for the duration of the trip. Because most of the tourists are from overseas, all of your couriers can speak at least two foreign languages as follows: Phil can speak French, German, Italian and Russian; Sue can speak Russian, French and Japanese; Duleep can speak Spanish and Greek; Trish can speak French, German, Italian and Greek; Wavell can speak French and Spanish; Amanda can speak Italian and Greek. On a particular day, you must organize six coach trips for a party of Japanese, a party of Russians, a party of Spanish, a party of French, a party of Germans and a party of Italians. All of the coach tours are scheduled to take place simultaneously. **Who will be the courier for the French party?**

| | | |
|---|---|---|
| A = Phil | B = Sue | C = Duleep |
| D = Trish | E = Wavell | F = Amanda |

## Question 2

You are a club secretary who has the job of making the arrangements for a day excursion. The members have been given the details of five possibilities, called A, B, C, D and E, and have been asked to place them in their order of preference. When the results are analysed it is found that they can be arranged into eight groups. The table below shows the order of preference of each of the eight groups of club members. It is not possible to arrange all five excursions, but the committee has decided that it will be possible to arrange two. As club secretary you have been told to choose the two that will allow every member to have either their first or their second choice. **Which two excursions will you choose?**

A B C D E

| Groups of club members | Excursions in order of preference | | | | |
|---|---|---|---|---|---|
| 1 | E | D | B | C | A |
| 2 | B | A | C | E | D |
| 3 | A | B | E | C | D |
| 4 | C | B | A | E | D |
| 5 | D | E | C | A | B |
| 6 | A | B | D | C | E |
| 7 | A | D | B | E | C |
| 8 | D | C | A | B | E |

# Examples from numerical reasoning tests

## Number problems

The examples given below are from a multiple-choice test in which you are presented with a fairly simple problem and required to select the correct answer from five possible answers. Number problem tests of this kind are based on the four basic arithmetical operations (addition, subtraction, division and multiplication); they also cover simple fractions, decimals and percentages applied to quantities of money, objects, speed, time and area. You are **not** allowed to use a calculator but you are permitted to use a sheet of paper or a notepad for any rough work. The sample questions given below should help you to get an idea of what is involved. In each case, record your answer by putting A, B, C, D or E in the box provided.

## Question 3

How much money would it cost to buy seven loaves of bread at 52p a loaf?

| A | B | C | D | E |
|---|---|---|---|---|
| £3.44 | £3.54 | £3.64 | £3.74 | £3.84 |

Answer = ☐

## Question 4

If I pay £4.56 for a tin of paint and 85p for a brush, how much will I have spent in total?

| A | B | C | D | E |
|---|---|---|---|---|
| £5.31 | £5.41 | £5.51 | £5.61 | £5.71 |

Answer = ☐

## Question 5

Two out of every eight cyclists are questioned in a spot check. Out of 408 cyclists, how many are questioned?

| A | B | C | D | E |
|---|---|---|---|---|
| 102 | 100 | 88 | 80 | 40 |

Answer = ☐

## Question 6

A worker's shift begins at 05.30 and lasts for 9 hours. What time does it end?

| A | B | C | D | E |
|---|---|---|---|---|
| 15.30 | 15.00 | 14.30 | 14.00 | 13.30 |

Answer = ☐

## Question 7

If my bus journey takes 35 minutes and my train journey takes 55 minutes, how long is my journey in total?

| A | B | C | D | E |
|---|---|---|---|---|
| 1½ hours | 1¼ hours | 70 minutes | ¾ hour | 85 minutes |

Answer = ☐

## Data interpretation

Because it is such a widely used skill both in the workplace and in connection with training and education courses, selectors are always interested in how well people can interpret data. In these tests you are given a series of statistical tables, graphs or diagrams followed by questions related to each data set. For each question there are five possible answers A–E. Your task is to work out which is the correct answer to each question, using the data provided, and without the use of a calculator. Now work your way through the sample questions provided below, recording your answer by putting A, B, C, D or E in the box provided.

## Question 8

The following table shows the price of fuel for heating in pence per useful kilowatt-hour:

| Fuel | pence |
|---|---|
| Butane (room heater) | 4.6 |
| Electricity (fan heater) | 5.2 |
| Kerosene (central heating) | 2.9 |
| Gas (wall heater) | 1.7 |
| Coal (open fire) | 3.5 |
| Anthracite (central heating) | 2.2 |

Which heating fuel is approximately twice the price of gas?

| A | B | C | D | E |
|---|---|---|---|---|
| Butane | Electricity | Kerosene | Coal | Anthracite |

Answer = ☐

## Question 9

The following table shows the number of emergencies attended by six Fire Service sub-stations during a five-month period:

| Sub-station | May | June | July | Aug | Sept |
|---|---|---|---|---|---|
| A | 11 | 10 | 12 | 26 | 27 |
| B | 22 | 23 | 20 | 42 | 28 |
| C | 36 | 46 | 58 | 68 | 43 |
| D | 21 | 22 | 24 | 27 | 26 |
| E | 16 | 16 | 15 | 19 | 12 |
| F | 24 | 18 | 26 | 37 | 29 |

What was the total number of emergencies attended by all six sub-stations in June and July?

| A | B | C | D | E |
|---|---|---|---|---|
| 283 | 309 | 290 | 310 | 287 |

Answer = ☐

## Comparison of quantities

This kind of test requires you to make a comparison between two quantities, X and Y. For some exercises, additional information is given that should be used in your determination of quantity. You are asked to record your answer by putting a tick in the appropriate box as follows:

A If the quantity at X is greater than the quantity at Y.
B If the quantity at Y is greater than the quantity at X.
C If the quantities at X and Y are equal.
D If insufficient information is given to make the comparison.

Given below are two questions for you to attempt.

## Question 10

You are dealt four cards from a well-shuffled standard pack of playing cards (which may contain a joker).

X The probability of being dealt four queens
Y The probability of being dealt the 6, 7, 8 and 9 of spades

A ☐ B ☐ C ☐ D ☐

## Question 11

X The percentage increase in council tax represented by a change from £60 per month to £80 per month
Y 25%

A ☐ B ☐ C ☐ D ☐

## Number sequences

There are selectors – not all – who want to know how adept you are at working with numbers. To find out, they may well put you through what is known as a 'number sequence test'. You will find that, in this type of test, each question is presented in the form of a line that contains a sequence of numbers, but where one number is missing and has been replaced with an 'xx'. In all cases the answer is a two-digit number. Your task is to work out that missing number. Given below are three worked examples to give an idea of what is involved. When you have studied them, try to do the sample questions that follow. Record your answers in the answer boxes provided.

## Examples

**1.** 3 7 11 xx 19 Answer = 15
**2.** 1 2 4 8 xx Answer = 16
**3.** 6 1 7 12 3 15 2 10 xx Answer = 12

In **Example 1**, the numbers increase by +4:

3 (+4) = 7 (+4) = 11 (+4) = **15** (+4) = 19

The missing number (or xx), therefore, is 15.

In **Example 2**, the numbers increase by a factor of 2 as follows:

1 (×2) = 2 (×2) = 4 (×2) = 8 (×2) = **16**

The missing number (or xx), therefore, is 16.

In **Example 3**, the numbers are in groups of three and, in each group of three, the second number added to the first equals the third. So:

6 + 1 = 7; 12 + 3 = 15; 2 + 10 = **12**

The missing number (or xx), therefore, is 12.

### Question 12

3 10 xx 24 31

xx = ☐

### Question 13

24 19 15 xx 10

xx = ☐

### Question 14

2 4 12 xx 240

xx = ☐

### Question 15

7 15 23 26 23 xx 7

xx = ☐

### Question 16

3 5 9 17 xx

xx = ☐

## Examples from verbal usage and reasoning tests

### Missing words

In this type of verbal reasoning test you will find sentences in which two gaps have been left. Your task is to decide what those missing words are. Below each sentence you will find four pairs of words, with a letter (A, B, C and D) above each pair. You have to work out which pair of words fits into the spaces correctly. Sometimes it is a question of the spelling of the words or their meaning. At other times it is a matter of the correct use of grammar. In some of the items the right answer will be 'None of these', in which case you would record your decision by writing the letter E in the answer box provided. The sample questions given below should help you to get the idea.

## Question 17

Three senior managers ________ present at the ________.

| A | B | C | D |
|---|---|---|---|
| was | was | were | were |
| enquirey | enquiry | enquiry | enquirey |

E None of these

Answer = ☐

## Question 18

A witness was ________ talking to the ________.

| A | B | C | D |
|---|---|---|---|
| scene | seen | scene | scene |
| suspect | susspect | susspect | suspect |

E None of these

Answer = ☐

## Mixed sentences

Just as some selectors want to know how skilful you are at dealing with numbers, others (probably most) want to know how competent you are with the English language and how adept you are at using it. In a certain form of verbal reasoning test you are given a series of sentences in which the positions of **two** words have been interchanged so that the sentences no longer make sense. You have to read each sentence carefully, pick out the two words and then underline them in pencil. The example given below should help you to understand what you have to do. When you have studied it, try the sample questions given below.

## Example

Some planning developments permit householders to carry out whatever authorities they wish.

**Answer:** The sentence should read: 'Some planning authorities permit householders to carry out whatever developments they wish.' So to record your answer the two words you would underline in the sentence are: <u>developments</u> and <u>authorities</u>.

## Question 19

Even when exhausted and afloat, a person will remain unconscious until he can be rescued, provided he is wearing a life jacket.

## Question 20

The snow on the greatest summits of the Alps, the lakes with their deep blue water and the woods full of flowers are among some of the highest beauties of nature.

## Question 21

We shall have cold salad at 9 o'clock; there will be cold meat, supper, sandwiches, fruit, sweets and trifle.

## Question 22

Too much rain ruins the crops, if they are also poor but it does not rain at all.

## Question 23

Before children start school in the UK at five years they must be six while going to school in Italy.

## Word links

Here is another kind of test that aims to probe your verbal facility. Your task is to identify two words in the **lower line, one in each half**, which, when paired with the words in the upper line, form what is called a 'verbal analogy'. Put simply, a verbal analogy is an agreement or similarity in the meaning of words. The two examples given below will give an idea of what you have to do in this type of test. When you have worked your way through them, try to do the sample questions provided.

### Example 1

| | | FISH | WATER | | |
|---|---|---|---|---|---|
| fin | bird | trout | sand | air | sea |

In this case **bird** and **air** are the correct answers because birds are found in the air in the same way as fish are found in water. With this type of analogy the general rule is: 'the top left word is to the top right word as a bottom left word is to a bottom right word'.

### Example 2

| | | HANGAR | GARAGE | | |
|---|---|---|---|---|---|
| field | engineer | plane | mechanic | car | house |

Here **plane** and **car** are the correct answers since a plane is kept in a hangar, just as a car is kept in a garage. With this type of analogy the general rule is: 'the top left word is to a bottom left word as the top right word is to a bottom right word'.

When tackling the sample questions below you should note that the correct answers always conform to one of the two general rules identified above – you will have to work out for yourself which one is used in each question. You should record your answer to each question by **underlining** in pencil the **two words** you have chosen.

## Question 24

| | | COURT | LAW | | |
|---|---|---|---|---|---|
| church | service | vicar | hymns | religion | tennis |

## Question 25

| | | BOOK | READER | | |
|---|---|---|---|---|---|
| paper | text | radio | listener | news | signal |

## Question 26

| | | FLOWERS | VASE | | |
|---|---|---|---|---|---|
| paint | mural | picture | canvas | frame | compost |

## Question 27

| | | FLOOR | CARPET | | |
|---|---|---|---|---|---|
| mattress | settee | rug | sheet | pullover | pillowcase |

## Question 28

| | | PEOPLE | LIBRARY | | |
|---|---|---|---|---|---|
| cow | book | individual | dairy | diary | book |

## Hidden sentences

Just to prove that selectors really do think verbal facility is important, they sometimes like to use another kind of test known as 'hidden sentences'. Here each question consists of a single sentence to which have been added a number of irrelevant words. These words are scattered throughout the sentence in order to make it 'hidden'. Your task is to discover that hidden sentence. So, what you have to do is to read through each question carefully in order to decide what the sentence should be. Then you have to indicate the **first three**

**words** and the **last three words** of the sentence by **underlining** them in pencil. To help you check that you have identified the sentence correctly, the number of words in the original sentence is given in brackets at the end of the item, eg '(12)'. It is necessary to count the words very carefully to ensure that you do not make a mistake. A sentence is only acceptable if it contains exactly the number of words indicated in the brackets. Where hyphens occur (eg 'five-year'), count two words. The following example should help you to understand what you have to do. When you have studied it, work your way through the sample questions provided.

## Example

with because the advent of new television ratings created
a exciting revolution in leisure days patterns of hobbies (10)

**Answer:** The original sentence was: 'The advent of television created a revolution in leisure patterns.'

In the test, therefore, you should mark your answer like this:

with because <u>the</u> <u>advent</u> <u>of</u> new television ratings created
a exciting revolution <u>in</u> <u>leisure</u> days <u>patterns</u> of hobbies (10)

In other words, you should underline the **first three words** in the sentence (ie 'the', 'advent' and 'of') and the **last three words** in the sentence (ie 'in', 'leisure' and 'patterns').

## Question 29

keep out this polythene around in out of length reach
of also and children if to not avoid the baby having
danger of the suffocation (14)

## Question 30

when they this product is obsolete using manufactured by after from 100% recycled paper writing and will uses some no wood pulp fiction (13)

## Question 31

in fact we make up blurs with stories fiction when in this documentary focusing about two a cameraman who comes from search (10)

## Question 32

at one the of talk I found out why it difficult how to understand concentration and some so lost gave interest sharing together (10)

## Question 33

making an studies game of fun while children playing up suggests games that in themselves there are too three causes also enjoyment of conflict (12)

## Sentence sequences

Finally, if you can stand yet another type of verbal reasoning test, here is one called 'sentence sequences'. In this type of test, you are given a series of prose passages, each consisting of four sentences. In each case the original order of the sentences has been changed. In other words, they are now out of sequence. Your task is to read each passage and work out what the correct sequence should be. In tests of this type you should:

- Begin by reading through the sentences in each question to get the sense of the passage.

- Then work out the correct sequence of the sentences, ie the order in which they were originally written.
- Use the numbers (1 to 4) given in brackets at the front of the sentences to record the correct sequence in the answer boxes provided.

The following example should help you to understand what to do. When you have studied it, try to answer the sample questions given below.

## Example

(1) There you will be issued with the key to your bedroom and your training folder. (2) This will normally be in the same building as the reception and your bedroom. (3) Upon arrival at the training centre please book in at reception. (4) The folder will contain a list of the training rooms and, having deposited your luggage in your room, you should go to the first training room listed.

**Answer:** To make sense the passage should read as follows:

(3) Upon arrival at the training centre please book in at reception. (1) There you will be issued with the key to your bedroom and your training folder. (4) The folder will contain a list of the training rooms and, having deposited your luggage in your room, you should go to the first training room listed. (2) This will normally be in the same building as the reception and your bedroom.

The **correct sequence**, therefore, is: 3, 1, 4 and 2, which you would record in the **answer boxes** as follows:

Answer 1 = [3]   2 = [1]   3 = [4]   4 = [2]

## Question 34

(1) It is, however, the longest way and if you do not need to go there I would suggest that you go the other way. (2) One route would take you down past the Post Office. (3) I would advise you to take that one if you need to conduct any business there. (4) There are two ways in which you can get to the supermarket from here.

Answer 1 = ☐ 2 = ☐ 3 = ☐ 4 = ☐

## Question 35

(1) Confidential records will then be kept but no names or addresses will be recorded on them, only a number that the staff will allocate to users of the service. (2) Yes, totally. (3) At first, a verbal contract will be made between the client and staff member. (4) Is the service confidential?

Answer 1 = ☐ 2 = ☐ 3 = ☐ 4 = ☐

## Question 36

(1) The Commission's chairperson, in presenting the report, commented that wider and more effective anti-discrimination legislation was necessary. (2) The demands came as the Commission presented its annual report, which records evidence of widespread discrimination. (3) Demands for a tough new racial discrimination law were made today, amid warnings of an end to the fragile peace in Britain's inner cities. (4) Specifically, the Commission for Racial Equality wants measures to prevent racial discrimination to be extended to central and local government.

Answer 1 = ☐ 2 = ☐ 3 = ☐ 4 = ☐

# Comprehension/critical thinking

Now the emphasis switches from verbal facility to understanding. In a comprehension test you are given several prose passages, each of which is followed by a set of questions or incomplete statements related to its content. After reading a passage, your task is to choose, from the alternatives given, the best answer or answers to each question, or the best ending to the statement. In each case you are told the number, one or two, of answers required. In the sample item given below you will find an extract of text, which is followed by two questions (A and B), each of which in turn offers you five choices (1–5). Your task is to read the text and then answer the questions by putting ticks (✓) alongside what you consider to be the correct choices.

## Question 37

For almost 30 years after it first captured nearly half of the global market, Japan dominated world shipbuilding. Even during the decade when the decline in the shipbuilding industry in other countries had been exacerbated by the entry of South Korea into the international market, Japan managed to hold on to its position. However, the cost it had to pay for this was high. Japan's shipbuilding companies had to lower their capacity by over one-third and to reduce their workforce by almost as much as their counterparts in the UK. This created particular difficulties for Japan's big shipbuilders, because of their commitment to providing their employees with employment for life. Although some of the workforce who were surplus to requirements could be redeployed in new industries and many others could be retired, it was difficult to cater for them all by these means and the guarantee of employment for life, so crucial in the industrial life of Japan, was put at risk.

A The decline in Japan's shipbuilding industry has
(2 answers)

1 been equal to that in the UK
2 occurred despite the increase in its share of the world market
3 resulted in a lowering of the costs of production
4 had high economic and social costs
5 threatened industrial relations in the country

B The world decline in shipbuilding was
(1 answer)

1 caused by Japan sustaining its output levels
2 a result of Japan's policy of employment for life
3 caused by vigorous marketing by the South Koreans
4 caused by a general decline in the demand for new vessels
5 the result of Japan's continued dominance of world markets

## Data sufficiency

These tests consist of exercises in which you are given a question and two statements, labelled (1) and (2), which give certain information. You are asked to decide whether the information given in the two statements is sufficient to answer the question, either separately or in combination.

Using your everyday knowledge of the world and mathematics, plus the information given in the statements, choose **one** of A, B, C, D or E as follows:

A If statement 1 ALONE is sufficient, but statement 2 alone is not sufficient to answer the question.
B If statement 2 ALONE is sufficient, but statement 1 alone is not sufficient to answer the question.
C If BOTH statements 1 and 2 TOGETHER are sufficient to answer the question, but NEITHER statement ALONE is sufficient.

D If EACH statement ALONE is sufficient to answer the question.

E If statements 1 and 2 together are NOT sufficient to answer the question asked.

Now try to answer the two questions given below.

## Question 38

Jersey potatoes cost twice as much as salad potatoes, which in turn are more expensive than baking potatoes. How much per kilo are Jersey potatoes?

1 Salad potatoes cost 10p per kilo more than baking potatoes.
2 Salad potatoes cost 30p per kilo.

Answer = ☐

## Question 39

What is the distance from one corner of a square field to the diagonally opposite corner?

1 The area of the field is 62,500 square metres.
2 The distance all the way round the field is 1,000 metres.

Answer = ☐

## Data evaluation

There are tests (notably one called the Watson–Glaser) that call for consideration of a series of propositions (either an inference, an assumption, a conclusion or an argument) relating to a given statement. If you are asked to take one of these tests, your job is to study the statements and then to evaluate how appropriate or valid each of these propositions is by answering **true** or **false**. Here is an example:

Only women can bear children. All women can bear children.

Question: Is the second assertion **true** or **false**?

Evidently the answer is false because there will be women who through some condition or other cannot bear children. We could give you some more of these questions to sample, but they would only take you so far because the range of subject matter that can be used to construct tests of this kind is enormous.

Suppose it is impossible to say whether a conclusion is true or false? In these circumstances it makes sense (since it reflects reality) to allow a third answer – 'impossible to say'. So we are talking now about an answering system that operates as follows:

A The conclusion is **true** given the situation described and the facts that are known about it.

B The conclusion is **false** given the situation described and the facts that are known about it.

C It is **impossible to say** whether the conclusion is true or false given the situation described and the facts that are known about it.

In order to get a better idea of what you have to do, take a look at the example given below.

- Read the information provided.
- Evaluate each of the five conclusions.
- Using a pencil, mark your answer A, B or C in the answer boxes provided.
- Check your answers against those provided below.

## Example

Ollie Jones and Ben Wilson, both aged 10, were reported missing at 20.00 after they failed to return home from a cycle ride to some nearby woods. The police have set up a search party for the two missing boys. The following facts are known:

- The woods are very dense and over 10 hectares in area.
- The two boys were admitted to a local hospital at 17.00.
- Ollie lived with his stepmother.
- Ben was an only child living with his father.
- Ben had a new 10-gear racing bike.
- The wood has several ponds and swampy areas.
- The older students picked on Ollie at school.
- Ben saw an educational psychologist at school each week.

The two boys could have run away from home. ☐

The two boys had a cycle accident and were taken to hospital. ☐

The older students had picked on Ollie in the woods. ☐

Ben had no brothers or sisters. ☐

Ben had no problems at school or at home. ☐

**Answers:** 1 = A 2 = C 3 = C 4 = A 5 = B

Here are two sample questions – the answers are given at the end of the chapter.

## Question 40

At 16.05 on Sunday 3 June an elderly man was found dead in Cuthbert Park. His right wrist had been slashed. The park-keeper had seen a young man running out of the park at 15.30. The following facts are known:

- The park had been shut for major landscaping work.
- The young man was employed by the landscape contractors and worked in the park.
- The dead man had been diagnosed with terminal cancer on Friday 1 June.
- The landscape contractors do not work on Sundays.
- The park-keeper is profoundly deaf.
- A sharp knife with a 16-centimetre blade was found 100 metres from the dead body.
- The victim was right-handed.

The park-keeper heard a scream from inside the park at 15.25 on Sunday 3 June. ☐

The victim may have committed suicide. ☐

The young man seen running out of the park had just clocked off from his work with the landscape contractors. ☐

The knife found 100 metres from the body had been used to slash the victim's wrist. ☐

The victim had been mugged and stabbed by the young man. ☐

## Question 41

A 19-year-old male was found unconscious in his flat on 28 December at 23.00. He was taken immediately to hospital where his stomach was pumped. Although he regained consciousness he died shortly afterwards. Neighbours recall seeing various young people going into the flat at all hours of the day and night. The following facts are known:

- Jake Pratt was a heroin addict.
- Empty bottles of spirits and paracetamol were found in the flat.
- Joe Horrocks supplied Jake with hard drugs.
- Jake used to frequent the local nightclub.
- Joe was the father of a two-month-old child.
- Joe's child was in care and had tested HIV positive.
- The victim was a compulsive gambler.
- The victim had bruises on his head.

The victim was homeless. ☐

Jake died of an overdose of drugs. ☐

Neighbours may have seen Joe enter the flat where the victim was found. ☐

The victim's child was in care. ☐

The neighbours took the victim to hospital. ☐

As you can imagine, there are tests that extend the **true** or **false** format even further. One variety invites you to answer according to an expanded format, eg **Definitely True, Probably True, Probably False** and **Definitely False.** You could say that the 'impossible to say' option has been finessed as between 'probably true' and 'probably false'. As with the last variety, the added complexity that has been introduced is deliberate and is designed to reflect the true reality of decision making that is demanded in the real world whether it be in the workplace or in an educational environment.

Here is a sample question around a fictitious organization.

## Question 42

**Memo**

From: Human Resources Directorate

To: District Managers

Some managers have started to question the validity of the preference surveys they are asked to administer to visitors to their sites. In particular there is a concern that visitors overstate their preference for on-site canteens in relation to the actual use made of the facilities. These managers want to reduce the numbers of staff they have employed there in order to relieve the genuine pressure on staff working in other areas. There is also a feeling on their part that canteen staff have more downtime than other people on the site.

Read the following statements and in each decide whether it is:

A Definitely True
B Probably True
C Probably False
D Definitely False

Record your answers to each question (A, B, C or D) in the boxes provided.

Not all managers believe that the preference surveys reflect a true picture of visitors' preferences. ☐

More visitors use the canteen facilities than would be expected from their responses to the preference surveys. ☐

If given a chance some managers would move staff to other areas. ☐

The canteen facilities are underused. ☐

There is no more pressure on staff working in one area than another. ☐

Visitors are aware that they do not use the canteen facilities as much as they say they will. ☐

What you need to do when taking tests of this type is to have your wits about you. That is generally true, of course (definitely not false), of all tests but particularly true (definitely true) of these verbal reasoning varieties. To help you sharpen up your wits you might want to look at the Kogan Page books *How to Pass Verbal Reasoning Tests* by Harry Tolley and Ken Thomas, and *The New Police Selection System* by Harry Tolley, Billy Hodge and Catherine Tolley. Don't be put off by the reference to police; Chapter 6 of this book is full of interesting verbal reasoning questions of the true/false/impossible to say type that will help you with plain true/false tests and other variations of them.

# Examples of situational judgement tests

## Question 43

Of the people who report to you, one, a man aged 40, is due for an annual salary review. Your line manager calls you into her office, and tells you that your colleague is not going to receive a pay increase on the grounds that he has not performed his duties to a sufficiently high standard to deserve a rise. You are surprised because you think that he has not noticeably underperformed. When you give him the bad news he says he has not done anything differently over the past year, and when he leaves he is clearly distressed. Choose two answers from A to D by putting a tick (✓) in the appropriate box to indicate what you think would be the **most** effective way of dealing with this situation, and a cross (✕) to indicate the **least** effective.

A Sympathize with your colleague saying that he hasn't been all that poor, and that if it had been left to you he would have had a pay rise – albeit small.

B Say that you don't like to have to convey this sort of news to a colleague, but that you are only the messenger.

C Observe that the decision was arrived at by using criteria applied to all employees, and that he is not the only one to have been given a zero rating (although you are careful not to mention any other names).

D Note that this is the first time he has been rated zero (which is true), that he still has a job and that in the past you have also been treated in this way.

A ☐ B ☐ C ☐ D ☐

## Question 44

Some of your colleagues have fallen into the habit of drifting in to work late – and the trend is for this to get progressively later. When challenged they tell you, some more vehemently than others, that what matters is not punctuality and attendance but performance and that, as far as they are concerned, they are performing to the required standard. Choose two answers from A to D by putting a tick (✓) in the appropriate box to indicate what you think would be the **most** effective way of dealing with this situation, and a cross (X) to indicate the **least** effective.

A Ask them what is wrong with expecting both attendance and performance from employees.

B Say that however much they believe they are performing well, and you are not necessarily disputing that, their lax time-keeping sets a poor example to other, perhaps less talented, colleagues.

C Observe that outward signs of laxity in a person's behaviour at work – and you would include habitual lateness in that – point to a lack of commitment.

D Say that while you would regret having to do it, this may become a disciplinary matter unless there is a discernible improvement in their time-keeping.

A ☐ B ☐ C ☐ D ☐

## Question 45

You are disturbed to find out that your manager has nominated everyone in your work group except you, to go on an important training course. Choose two answers from A to D by putting a tick (✓) in the appropriate box to indicate what you think would be the **most** effective way of dealing with this situation, and a cross (X) to indicate the **least** effective.

A Assume that it was simply a mistake of some kind and find an occasion to draw your manager's attention to it.
B Discuss the matter with your manager explaining why you think you too should go on this course along with your colleagues.
C Make a complaint to the Head of Human Resources about how you have been unfairly treated.
D Write and hand in a letter of resignation.

A ☐ B ☐ C ☐ D ☐

## Question 46

It is patently obvious that two members of your workplace team (call them P and Q) do not get on with each other. Their mutual antipathy is having an adverse impact on the performance of the whole team insofar as no one is willing to take on a collaborative task in which the two of them are involved. Choose two answers from A to D by putting a tick (✓) in the appropriate box to indicate what you think would be the **most** effective way of dealing with this situation, and a cross (X) to indicate the **least** effective.

A Implore your manager to knock their heads together.
B Assuming there is someone in the team who is friendly with both P and Q, ask that person to broker peace between them.
C Keep a diary on the spats between P and Q and then share it with them at a meeting where you ask them to promise to stop squabbling.
D Say to P and Q – to their faces – that if they dislike each other so much why doesn't one of them request a transfer out of the team.

A ☐ B ☐ C ☐ D ☐

### Question 47

At the conclusion of your annual appraisal interview you are asked to identify what you regard as your biggest weakness, which you need to address in your personal development plan. Choose two answers from A to D by putting a tick (✓) in the appropriate box to indicate what you think would be the **most** effective way of dealing with this situation, and a cross (X) to indicate the **least** effective.

A That you ask too much of yourself and in that respect you are your own worst enemy.
B That on occasions you struggle to prioritise the conflicting demands on your time.
C That because of your high standards, you ask too much of others so that when they come up short of your expectations you get disappointed.
D That you feel you could contribute more in team meetings, but that this is something you are already working on.

A ☐ B ☐ C ☐ D ☐

## The importance of doing well in selection tests

Increasingly, a good performance on tests such as the ones described above is important in securing employment or access to further training or to desirable courses of study. Although it will not be the only performance you are judged on it may just determine, for example, whether or not you are asked to proceed to the later stages of an assessment centre or multi-assessment event. Some or all of the following may help to offset a modest performance on a psychometric test:

- the strength of your formal qualifications;
- your previous work and life experience as reflected in your CV;
- the way you perform in an interview;
- how well you cope with the other exercises you are asked to undertake.

It goes without saying that an outstanding test score may not be sufficient to compensate for serious weaknesses detected elsewhere in the assessment process, but don't let that stop you doing your level best on the psychometric tests.

## Practice does make a difference

Experience strongly suggests that many candidates fail to reflect their ability in selection tests both because they are over-anxious and – the two are connected – because they have not known what to expect. Regular practice will also give you the opportunity to work under conditions similar to those you will experience when taking real tests. In particular, you should become accustomed to working under the pressure of the strict time limits imposed in real test situations. Familiarity with the demands of the tests and working under simulated test conditions should help you to cope better with any nervousness you experience when taking tests that really matter. The old adage that 'practice makes perfect' may not have been coined in connection with selection tests, but it certainly can make a difference – and always for the better! Remember that practising to take tests is essentially a solo activity, which means you can do it whenever and wherever you like, and as often as you like. None of the other assessment exercises described in this book are easier to practise for – so you really have no excuse.

It has been impossible in the space available within this book to give you more than an introduction to some of the main types of psychometric tests that you might encounter at an assessment centre and to provide you with a small number of sample questions for you to try out for yourself. If, when you have been through the material, you decide that you need more practice you would be well advised to consult some of the other books in the Kogan Page series (see **Further reading from Kogan Page**). Many of these texts have been specially written for the purpose of providing practice tests designed to help you develop your ability to cope with cognitive tests of different types. You should also make sure to practise on whatever online tests you can find. Some websites are given later in the chapter.

## Performing to the best of your ability on tests

If you want to perform to the best of your ability on psychometric tests the advice given below is well worth following:

- Make sure that you know what you have to do before you start – if you do not understand, ask the supervisor.
- Read the instructions carefully before the test starts in order to make sure that you understand them.
- Skim-reading through this part of the test is not good enough – it can cause you to overlook important details and to make mistakes that are easily avoidable.
- Even if you have taken a test before, don't assume that the instructions (and the worked examples) are the same as last time – they may have been changed. Read them as carefully as you can.
- If it helps, highlight or underline the 'command words' in the instructions, ie those words that tell you what you have to do.
- Once the test begins, work as quickly and accurately as you can. Remember, every unanswered question is a scoring opportunity missed!

- Check frequently to make sure that the question you are answering matches the space you are filling in on the answer grid. It is possible to get out of sequence and you can lose valuable time retrieving yourself.
- Avoid spending too much time on questions you find difficult – leave them and go back later if you have time.
- If you are uncertain about an answer, enter your best-reasoned choice (but try to avoid simply 'guessing').
- If you have any time left after you have answered all the questions, go back and check through your answers.
- Keep working as hard as you can throughout the test – the more correct answers you get the higher your score will be.
- Concentrate your mind on the test itself and nothing else – you cannot afford to allow yourself to be distracted.
- Be positive in your attitude – don't allow previous failures in tests and examinations to have a detrimental effect on your performance on this occasion. In other words, don't allow yourself to be beaten before you begin!

You can begin to put this advice into effect by using the practice tests available via the sources listed in **Further reading from Kogan Page**. Used systematically, these should help you to establish good habits, which will serve you well when you come to take real tests at an assessment centre or multi-assessment event.

## Completing psychometric tests online

There is nothing to worry about in doing electronic versions of tests – you might even find them to be more fun than the paper and pencil versions. Obviously we are not in a position here to simulate and therefore prepare you for the experience, but why not go to the web to complete a practice test or two? Useful university careers department sites (which have links to other sites) are:

- www.careers.ed.ac.uk
- www.bath.ac.uk/careers/development/tests
- www.nd.ac.uk/careers/jobs/applications/assessment/
- www.york.ac.uk/careers.

Other sites (most of which you will find listed in the four sites just mentioned) are:

- The Morrisby Organisation for tests including an emotional intelligence test (www.morrisby.com).
- Saville & Holdsworth (SHL) for verbal, numerical and diagrammatic reasoning tests (www.shldirect.com).
- Tests from Team Technology (www.teamtechnology.co.uk).
- The Watson–Glaser is available online through www.getfeedback.net.

If you aspire to join the Civil Service, and especially the fast stream, you might find yourself being invited to attend a Civil Service assessment centre. In that eventuality you will no doubt want to practise the Civil Service Fast Stream Qualifying Test. There are three tests: clerical, numerical and verbal reasoning. You can do these practice tests online by going to www.faststream.gov.uk/practice.

All in all, therefore, there are plenty of online practice opportunities for you to tap into. Our advice is that you should try to take every advantage of them in preparation for the psychometric tests you are likely to face at an assessment centre. You should also take a close look at the Kogan Page book authored by Mike Bryon.

# Answers to sample questions

## Logical reasoning

Question 1 E (Wavell)
Question 2 B and D

## Number problems

Question 3 C
Question 4 B
Question 5 A
Question 6 C
Question 7 A

## Data interpretation

Question 8 D (coal)
Question 9 C (290)

## Comparison of quantities

Question 10 C
Question 11 A (one-third is greater than 25%)

## Number sequences

Question 12 xx = 17
Question 13 xx = 12
Question 14 xx = 48
Question 15 xx = 15
Question 16 xx = 33

## Missing words

| | |
|---|---|
| Question 17 | C |
| Question 18 | E |

## Mixed sentences

| | |
|---|---|
| Question 19 | afloat; unconscious |
| Question 20 | greatest; highest |
| Question 21 | salad; supper |
| Question 22 | if; but |
| Question 23 | before; while |

## Word links

| | |
|---|---|
| Question 24 | church; religion |
| Question 25 | radio; listener |
| Question 26 | picture; frame |
| Question 27 | mattress; sheet |
| Question 28 | individual; book |

## Hidden sentences

| | |
|---|---|
| Question 29 | keep, this, polythene<br>danger, of, suffocation |
| Question 30 | this, product, is<br>no, wood, pulp |
| Question 31 | fact, blurs, with<br>about, a, cameraman |
| Question 32 | I, found, it<br>so, lost, interest |
| Question 33 | studies, of, children<br>causes, of, conflict |

## Sentence sequences

Question 34 1 = 4; 2 = 2; 3 = 3; 4 = 1
Question 35 1 = 4; 2 = 2; 3 = 3; 4 = 1
Question 36 1 = 3; 2 = 4; 3 = 2; 4 = 1

## Comprehension/critical thinking

Question 37 A = 2 and 4; B = 4

## Data sufficiency

Question 38 The answer is B. You only need statement 2 to work out the price of Jersey potatoes.
Question 39 The answer is D. From either statement you can work out that the length of each side of the field is 250 metres, after which it remains to calculate the diagonal as the hypotenuse of a right-angled triangle.

## Data evaluation

Question 40 1 = B; 2 = A; 3 = B; 4 = C; 5 = C
Question 41 1 = B; 2 = C; 3 = A; 4 = C; 5 = C
Question 42

1. A Definitely true – you are told as much in the memo (you would have to reject the managers' judgement calls if you were to answer differently).
2. C Probably false – there is no indication at all that it is true but you cannot be sure that it is definitely false.
3. A Definitely true – the memo says so.
4. B Probably true – again you cannot be certain.
5. D Definitely false – the memo talks about *genuine* pressure in other areas, suggesting that the pressure on canteen staff is not entirely genuine or at least is less than that on other staff.
6. B Probably true – you can never be sure what *all* visitors are aware of.

## Situational judgement tests: answer appraisal

**Question 43** Answer C is the most effective; answer A the least. With C you assure your colleague that the process is objective, and that he is not alone in the workforce. With alternative A you would look weak, too keen to 'buddy up', and insubordinate. This action would only open up fault-lines among the staff. The same is true to a lesser extent of alternative B.

**Question 44** Answer B is the most effective response; answer D the least effective. Superficially A looks attractive, but it is more a debating point and unlikely to lead to constructive action. Likewise answer C, which anyway is just an assertion. In choosing B you are making a statement about the importance of unity, and that breakaway groups operating by their own rules are not acceptable. In choosing D you would be issuing a threat, which should only be used as a last resort.

**Question 45** Answer A is the most effective response; answer D the least effective. By choosing A you are saying that you wish to hear the reason from the 'horse's mouth'. If what you hear is not what you want to hear, then at least you will have got to the bottom of the matter. By contrast, D is an impulsive response that accomplishes nothing – better to hear what your manager has to say first. In any case, it is a small matter in the overall scheme of things – there are always other training courses for you to go on.

**Question 46** Answer C is the most effective; answer A the least effective. By choosing C you are setting down evidence to which P and Q have to respond – hopefully in a constructive manner. If their differences cannot be resolved then perhaps it is time to move to D. Choice of A indicates an over-reliance on authority to solve the problem. Yes, that is partly what they are employed to do, and it could be argued that a good manager should not be allowed to let it fester, but this is essentially a problem for the team to resolve internally. The manager may issue a reprimand to P and Q, and they may be contrite (though one of them will probably be defiant) – but what good does that do if within a week they have regressed to where they were before? Once the other members of the team have shown where they stand, P and Q know that their colleagues now expect them to change their ways for the better. Choice of B puts the onus on one person – it is better if this problem is shared.

**Question 47** Answer D is the most effective; answer A the least effective. By choosing D you are admitting to having a weakness – maybe not a huge one – and that you are aware of it, and are already trying to do something to correct it. The manager might think that they could assist you in that regard, and that the weakness you have identified is not too serious anyway. Answers A and C are obviously not weaknesses at all. Of the two, A is the more egotistical and would seem to store up more problems for the future than C. In both cases the appraiser would be justified in concluding that here is a person who is unwilling to reveal or discuss their weaknesses.

5

# How to project yourself authentically through personality, motivation and emotional intelligence questionnaires

The **aims** of this chapter are to: explain why selectors choose to use personality questionnaires and inventories – these terms being treated as interchangeable; acquaint you with the rationale underpinning the design of personality questionnaires (PQs); introduce you to the most commonly used models of personality; advise you on how to present yourself through PQs; give you opportunities to work through some examples of the most commonly used questionnaires; and, most importantly, offer constructive suggestions on how to prepare for PQs. In the second part of the chapter we repeat the exercise for emotional intelligence questionnaires (EIQs) and motivation questionnaires. It is most unlikely that you will be given all three types of questionnaire – there won't be sufficient time and, besides, it would result in unnecessary duplication.

# Personality

In his film *Zelig*, Woody Allen tried to portray a man without a personality, when of course there is no such thing. We all have personalities and if we go to work (or a place of study) we take them with us. We might leave our brains at the gate (although we shouldn't) but we always take our personalities through with us. They then affect the way we work or approach training or study. A person who is always 'wound up' is likely to perform differently from a placid person; a person who is preoccupied with details is likely to act differently from a 'broad-brush' person.

## Why selectors use personality questionnaires

Understandably, selectors want to find out as much as they can about such individual differences – PQs help them to do that. The same applies to individual differences in emotional intelligence. Hence, to know how self-aware someone is, or how self-controlled, is of great interest to selectors – and, given the changing nature of work, training programmes and education courses, they will be equally interested in an applicant's motivation, empathy and social skills.

So, something we all experience – how people impact on us – tells us that it is always worth trying to get an assessment of personality, simply because it is too important to leave out of the selection equation. The people who are selecting you may not have rationalized it in precisely that way (or at all) but that is what is in their minds when, for example, they ask you to do a PQ or an EIQ.

## Personality is not the same as ability – at all

It is necessary at this point to distinguish between two kinds of mind measures: measures of maximum performance, which indicate what an applicant *can do*; and measures of typical performance, which indicate what an applicant is *likely to do* or would *prefer to do*.

Most ability tests (such as numerical, verbal or spatial reasoning tests) fall into the first category. Personality questionnaires belong to the second category. They are not tests of what a person can do because there are no right or wrong answers to the questions they pose. If you ask someone which of the following he or she would prefer to do: bungee jumping, needlework or collecting for charity, the answer you get is a preference – the person's preferred choice from the list of alternatives. The answer given, therefore, is neither right nor wrong. However, if you asked for the square root of 729 and the answer is anything other than 27, then it is wrong. It should also be noted that if the question is put as a forced choice – a preference between three options – the answer given has nothing to say about whether the person would enjoy his or her choice or be any good at it. So, just because we express a preference in a PQ does not mean that we like doing that thing. (Would you prefer to climb Mount Everest or K2, always supposing you could? Well, neither, actually!)

Consequently, unlike ability tests, PQs and EIQs are not objective – all they tell you about is a person's preferences. The results, therefore, can only be suggestive or allusive. Much depends on the skill of the test constructors in giving you options where the preferences you choose tell them something meaningful about you. PQs work on the basis that if you can probe away often enough into some aspect of behaviour a more or less coherent picture will begin to emerge of how a person is likely to behave in particular circumstances or under certain conditions. If selectors want to find out how outgoing you are likely to be, they will look at all of your answers to the items in the questionnaire that focus on your sociability – you will probably have noticed how much repetition there is if you have done PQs before. If there is a 'Would you prefer to spend a night at home with a good book or go out for a drink?' then sometime later in the PQ there is bound to be a question like 'At a party do you tend to get involved or stay on the fringes?'

Notice that the first question could be made more pointed by rephrasing it as 'Would you prefer to spend a night in with a good book or go out for a drink – even if you knew that none of your friends was likely to be there?' The scope for question designers to ratchet up questions in this way so as to squeeze out a little more authentic behaviour is considerable but, of course, they are constrained by the time they can take. Consequently there are rather long PQs and, as you might expect, they get rather tedious to complete. The trend is for shorter questionnaires where the designers hope to get as much useful information as they can in the shortest possible time. But, as you can appreciate, there is always a trade-off between time and the amount and quality of the data obtained and hence the reliability and validity of the outcomes.

## Opaque and transparent PQs

PQs can be broadly divided into those that are **transparent**, such as the Occupational Personality Questionnaire (OPQ), which contains questions closely (but not exclusively) related to the workplace, and those that are somewhat **opaque**, such as the California Personality Inventory (CPI). Transparent inventories have the advantage that you can see clearly the potential value of completing the questionnaire, but the disadvantage is that you can easily see what the questions are getting at. Opaque questionnaires contain questions that tend to be unrelated to the workplace – there used to be a question in the CPI, 'Do you prefer taking a bath to a shower?', and it is difficult to see what it is they are trying to get at. That means that it is tough to 'fake good', ie put forward a preferred (or even 'perfumed') view of yourself, but also that you, the candidate, may take some convincing of the value of completing the questionnaire.

The same applies to word association tests, like the Thomas International. Asking people to word-associate is a dubious practice at the best of times, given the great variation in how we respond to words. If you are in any doubt about this think of a word like 'smart' or 'cute' or 'winning'. What does 'cute' mean to you? Is it (a) smart, (b) winning or (c) nauseating? Not only is the English language over-engineered with meanings, but also our individual use of it is often so idiosyncratic that it is hard to see what sensible conclusions can be drawn from word association tests. If you happen to get one of these tests, the advice is to just 'grin and bear it'. It is unlikely that the results of one PQ will make the difference between success and failure at an assessment centre or a multi-assessment event.

## How to prepare for a PQ – why it is best to tell the truth

The headline message in this chapter is that you should make time before you take a PQ to think about your own 'occupational' personality. To do this properly, you will need the help of people who are close enough to you to know you well. As a first step, try to establish what your occupational personality is – roughly (or approximately) is probably the best you can expect to achieve. What you are being asked to do is to decide what personality you take with you when you go to work or to your place of training/study. This should enable your view of yourself to emerge from the PQ, rather than allow it to uncover your hidden personality on your behalf. After all, that is precisely what those who devise PQs expect to happen – if they have got their thinking right. They validate their instruments against accurate impressions of individual personalities offered by those who know us best. We realize that you may never have done a formal check on your personality, but most of us have a good idea of who we are – even though we have never articulated it. If you feel a little bit in the dark at this stage, don't panic – just start by asking yourself a few basic questions such as:

- Am I a party animal or somewhat inhibited?
- Am I a team player or an individualist?
- Do I let things get me down or am I able to put worries to one side?
- Am I happy to be told things or do I have to discover them for myself?

That is just for a start. Later we have exercises that are intended to help you arrive at a more detailed working model of your occupational personality. You could also take a careful look at the self-discovery exercise on pages 10–13 of Mark Parkinson's book *How to Master Personality Questionnaires* (published by Kogan Page).

Once you have got a skeletal outline of the core 'you', it is time to share your thoughts with people who know you well in order to see if they can corroborate and generally validate the conclusions you have reached about yourself. Once you have their input you can carry on with this process of clarifying who you are to yourself, so adding to the working model you are developing of your personality. If you have done PQs before and can remember the results and which parts of them you thought were really 'you', then you can factor that information into your working model. This model is what you should try to take with you when faced with a PQ at assessment centres or multiple assessment events. It is what you allow to generate your answers to individual questions. It is in your own best interest not to lie or to try to construct something that is inconsistent with your self-image as reflected in the model you have constructed.

Let us give you an example – it is about leadership. We might all like to think that we are leaders, but most of us have to accept that we are not. It is very tempting to give the impression that you are a leader, but highly dangerous when you know in your heart of hearts that you are not. Imagine having to explain in an interview that you are not really sure that you possess the leadership qualities you claimed to have. Remember that the interviewers are unlikely to have seen you before and will tend to look askance at any equivocation or shilly-shallying. You should also remember that if you decide to 'bluff it out' by insisting that you do indeed have leadership qualities (and can even concoct examples to bear out what you are saying) then you may well end up creating serious problems for yourself.

To illustrate what has been said above, here is what a PQ read-out had to say about one of the authors (referred to hereafter as X):

> *X is rather reserved and reflective in nature. He may like to have time for quiet concentration and be relatively self-sufficient. Probably he prefers a small number of close friends to a wider circle of acquaintances. He may be shy or find it difficult to initiate new social contacts, and may like time to think before acting. In meetings a relatively quiet front may mask a strong grasp of issues being discussed.*
>
> *He is an inquiring and questioning person who likes to place current experiences and events into a 'big picture' context. He is patient with theory, and ideas, and may feel they play an important role in driving change. He may put the emphasis on innovation rather than implementation, and be keen to learn new skills and make use of new techniques. He may be suspicious of 'fixit' solutions that fail to take account of underlying issues.*
>
> *X finds it hard to deal with the more frustrating events at work without feeling annoyance, or expressing this to others. He is emotionally responsive and may show some volatility in the face of upset. He may occasionally feel rather vulnerable or*

> *hurt when others express negative emotions or exchange views frankly, and may feel emotionally involved with his commitments at work.*

X felt that the PQ had captured salient aspects of his occupational personality. The transcript is neither damagingly critical, nor is it over-flattering – a balanced view, in fact, which is what a potential recruiter would want to receive. X's tendency to 'wear his heart on his sleeve', and his inability to dissimulate, has caused him some problems in the past, as have his relationships with 'authority'. He now understands that he can be too open, and that he must be prepared on occasions to 'bite his lip'. He also knows from experience that he must be careful in choosing those with whom he works. He is not a team player and would not dream now of applying for a position that requires intense teamwork, which is not to say that he has not done so in the past. Happily, most of us learn through our experiences – at least some of the time.

X would not have wanted the PQ read-out to say that he was outgoing or a social animal or, for that matter, a pragmatist, and would not have completed the PQ in a way that would knowingly have brought out such a snapshot of himself. An appreciation of what drives you is what you (and the selectors) need from a PQ report. If that proves to be a 'warts and all' picture, then so be it – that's how it should be.

Here is an extract from another report on X. Once again it is none too flattering, in an everyday sense, but in X's opinion it is not too far from the mark. This particular PQ seeks to bring to the surface so-called 'derailing' aspects of personality, ie those features of personality that if allowed to go unchecked or unchanged can cause havoc. 'Derailing' has always been common among top executives – you can no doubt think of some well-known examples. You can see why selectors are liable to find PQs of this kind to be the most instructive of all – not least because they are the most intrusive. However, they are not in universal use by any means so you may not encounter one. Out of interest, here is the relevant extract from X's report:

> *X received an elevated score on the charming–manipulative scale, suggesting that he may come across to others as quite charming, independent and self-assured. He is likely to be willing to make quick decisions, and may be described by others as bright, pleasure seeking and adventurous. Such elevated scores can sometimes have a negative side as the charming aspect of these social skills is eroded under pressure. People with elevated scores may be viewed as somewhat impulsive and risk-taking at times. They may also occasionally use their social skill to manipulate or even to deceive others.*

Of course 'charming' is not to be spurned, though no one likes being told that they might be 'manipulative'. The bottom line is that you have to accept observations of this kind in a feedback session. In any case you should already know things like this about yourself – or at least have more than an inkling of it. Otherwise, you are probably just deceiving yourself – and others. You can always tell people who prefer to give a perfumed account of themselves by their reactions when asked what is their worst fault. Our experience of questioning such people suggests that they are apt to say things like 'If only I could learn not to drive myself too hard.' Instead of faults they offer virtues, or even say it is nothing to do with them, such as 'I expect other people to be prepared to put in as much effort for the good of the team as I do.'

The value of self-knowledge should never be underestimated – we will have more to say about this when discussing emotional intelligence. You only have to look at some of the more catastrophic mismatches between people and jobs to realize that many of us do not possess a keen notion of who we are and what we are capable of. This gap between self-perception and ability to deliver is often most marked among politicians – we will leave it to you to think of some notable examples.

Why, you may be asking yourself, do recruiters not save themselves the bother of administering a PQ (or rather the chore of feeding back the results) when they could just ask you at interview what sort of person you are? Well, they may do that anyway, but the chief reason is that not all of us have worked ourselves out, ie have not arrived at a working model in the way we have been describing. In that case it is only fair to ask everyone to complete a PQ. It then becomes possible to use what the PQ throws up to explore the personalities of the less self-aware as well as the self-aware.

## Putting the results of a PQ into perspective

Because of the subjectivity arising from asking you to give preferences, selectors know that they cannot put too much weight on the results of PQs. That is one of the reasons why PQs are only one part of the total evidence that selectors consider when making their final judgements. Having said that, if you produce a profile of yourself, based on a PQ that you have completed, that you cannot substantiate in an interview, you could be creating difficulties for yourself.

The good news is that you will not succeed (or fail) at an assessment centre solely on the outcomes of a PQ. So make sure you shine on most of the other assessment exercises, and, if you do happen to get a PQ of the opaque variety, complete it as best you can. As for transparent questions, there really is no point in trying to 'gild the lily' because sooner or later you will be caught out – probably in the interview. You should also be aware that PQs themselves have traps built into them in order to catch out those who are being less than truthful. It really is in your best interests to reveal yourself sincerely as far as the questions require it. Think of it this way. If you were to perjure yourself in the way you represent your personality then it is odds on that you should not have been applying for that job in the first place.

## Models of personality

Those who devise PQs and analyse the results will interpret and report on your results in various ways, according to which model of personality they favour – back to preference again! Don't let this variety trouble you. You won't know it but they might be sizing you up in terms of a two-factor model, a five-factor model or even Type A versus Type B. If you want to know more check yourself out using the examples provided in the box below.

### Type A or Type B?

Do you know how to relax? Are you satisfied with the world around you? Are you competitive? Impatient? Hostile? Or are you laid-back? Chilled out? Placid? **Type A** personalities, the driven ones, are well used to stress. Those who fall into the **Type B** category are very different – they wish to avoid stress. In seeking recognizable achievement, Type A individuals are certainly putting themselves under pressure. They will say 'I want people to respect and admire me for what I've done' whereas a Type B person will say 'I want people to like me for who I am.'

To be a Type A is usually considered bad news. It is generally supposed your days are numbered – that stroke is just around the corner. So why not slow down? What's the hurry? But Type A personalities do not see it that way – far from it. 'Drive and energy', 'get-up-and-go' and 'can-do' – these are their watch-words. The slogan 'You can rest when you're dead' is cited with approval. What others perceive as weaknesses, they parade with pride. Ask Type As for their biggest single weakness and they will deliberate, cogitate and after an age (for them) come up with 'I do too much.'

Type Bs, with their laid-back, 'gone fishing' approach to life, are anathema to Type As, which is why it is such a productive dichotomy. Faced with a question on a PQ like 'I get angry when other people don't meet their goals', Type As will grimly answer 'True', just as they will readily answer 'False' to 'My enjoyment comes from playing Nice guys definitely come second – or nowhere at all.

Type A or Type B? You will know which you are – on the whole. But do not allow yourself to be too easily speared. When your Type A qualities are revealed, as they surely will be, strive to muddy the waters by, for instance, pointing out that when on holiday you are often Type B – a real lamb. It takes you no time at all to settle in, you never take the mobile or laptop, and basically you are sweetness and light. 'But what about waiters and holiday reps?' they ask, knowing that these characters are just lying in wait to 'ruin' a Type A's holiday. 'No problem,' you say, lying through your teeth (all Type As are forced to be 'economical with the truth' on occasion – there is too much to keep together).

Unfair as it may seem, Type Bs should expect to be attacked for what are seen as their saintly ways. 'Surely you must get angry,' Type As are apt to say in an attempt to bait them. Type As adore high-octane emotion whereas Type B individuals loathe it – though sometimes they cannot escape it. What you see then is a very slow burn that culminates in an explosion, or the nearest Type Bs come to an explosion. You know the emotion is there because it leaks in the form of long silences, glares, hissed remarks, snapped denials that anything is wrong – 'What's wrong? Nothing's wrong.'

Now that you have decided whether you are Type A or B, you can put that to one side and concentrate on determining where you stand on the list given below – this is what most PQs are seeking to establish:

- extrovert or introvert?
- stable or unstable (neurotic)?
- conscientious or corner-cutter?
- tolerant or authoritarian?
- thinker or feeler?

To help you decide which you are, look at the pairs of words listed in **Tables 5.1** to **5.5**. Put a tick (✓) in the box next to the word if you identify with it and a cross (✗) if you don't. In the case of **Table 5.1**, if you place more ticks alongside the words in the left-hand column than the right it suggests that you are an extrovert rather than an introvert. Repeat the exercise for **Tables 5.2** to **5.5**. Of course, in three cases at least the labels on the personality types on the left are more attractive than those on the right. So, it will be a good test of your honesty if you spurn the temptation to lean towards the left in making your choices – and if you have to face up to some 'home truths' in the process, it is better for that to happen at home than at a place where it might count.

**Table 5.1** Extrovert or introvert?

| **Extrovert** | **✓/✗** | **Introvert** | **✓/✗** |
|---|---|---|---|
| Assertive | | Withdrawn | |
| Excitement-seeking | | Shy | |
| Enthusiastic | | Loner | |
| Gregarious | | Reflective | |
| Talker | | Listener | |

**Table 5.2** Stable or unstable?

| **Stable** | ✓/✗ | **Unstable** | ✓/✗ |
|---|---|---|---|
| Calm | | Anxious | |
| Unruffled | | Angry | |
| Balanced | | Insecure | |
| Composed | | Changeable | |
| Sober | | Temperamental | |

**Table 5.3** Conscientious or corner-cutter?

| **Conscientious** | ✓/✗ | **Corner-cutter** | ✓/✗ |
|---|---|---|---|
| Dependable | | Unreliable | |
| Prudent | | Undisciplined | |
| Conformist | | Rebel | |
| Dutiful | | Erratic | |
| Detail-conscious | | Broad-brush | |

**Table 5.4** Tolerant or authoritarian?

| **Tolerant** | ✓/✗ | **Authoritarian** | ✓/✗ |
|---|---|---|---|
| Flexible | | Rigid | |
| Empathetic | | Domineering | |
| Tolerant | | Narrow | |
| Optimistic | | Forceful | |
| Liberal | | Dictatorial | |

**Table 5.5** Thinker or feeler?

| Thinker | ✓/✗ | Feeler | ✓/✗ |
|---|---|---|---|
| Abstract | | Sentimental | |
| Strategic | | Seat-of-the-pants | |
| Critical | | Emotional | |
| Rational | | Romantic | |
| Logical | | Intuitive | |

## Some examples of PQ questions for you to do

**Table 5.6** gives some typical PQ questions. The answer key you are asked to use is: Definitely disagree (**DD**); Disagree on balance (**DB**); Agree on balance (**AB**); Definitely agree (**DA**). You have to decide how you respond to statements like those in **Table 5.6**; have a go at answering them using the answer key given above.

**Table 5.6** Typical PQ questions

| Statement | DD | DB | AB | DA |
|---|---|---|---|---|
| I am hard to fool | | | | |
| If I see something wrong I have to speak out | | | | |
| I don't lose my rag like other people | | | | |
| I expect friends to let me down | | | | |
| It takes a lot to get me roused | | | | |
| I am a team player | | | | |
| I take my time to warm to people | | | | |
| I wear my heart on my sleeve | | | | |
| I am a private person | | | | |
| I have to work things out for myself | | | | |

How did you get on? Did you know enough about yourself to give an unequivocal answer to each question? How many Disagree on balance (DB) or Agree on balance (AB) answers did you give? Could these reflect your uncertainty about yourself?

Most of the well-known PQs can be tried online. Good places to go are the site for the Quintax PQ (www.quintax.co.uk) and the Psykey site (they do the tests that look at derailing characteristics), www.psykey.ltd.uk. You could also look at the sites mentioned at the end of Chapter 4.

## Emotional intelligence

The term 'emotional intelligence' (EI) has come into the language quite recently, but colloquialisms for aspects of EI have been in common use for far longer. You – we – come across them all the time. How often do we say that someone is a 'loose cannon' or is acting like a 'headless chicken'? Both of these commonly used expressions indicate that we think that the person's behaviour results from a lack of **self-control**. If you find yourself saying that someone can 'read you like a book' then that person is probably exhibiting strong **empathy**. To be cited as 'together' is a compliment, and signifies developed **self-awareness**. If you are reckoned to be 'a good mixer', then it is fair to suppose that you have well-developed **social skills**. If someone says of you that you 'don't let the grass grow under your feet' then it is likely that your **motivation** is being praised. These are the key elements that collectively constitute emotional intelligence (for much more read our book *Test Your Emotional Intelligence*, published by Kogan Page).

If you ever wonder why EQ should be taken seriously, consider what is involved in working or studying with other people. Plainly, having a good intellect as evidenced by academic qualifications is never going to be enough to guarantee success when the problems people present when they come together are essentially emotional in character. Everyone has experienced it, whether it was in the playground at school or in the workplace. P was hysterical, Q sulked if he didn't get his own way, R was prickly, S threw tantrums, T was flighty, U didn't respect V, W underachieved, X didn't like working with Y, Z was a bully – no doubt you could put names to each of these characteristic behaviours.

The ability to cope with the problems people create depends crucially on being able to manage your own emotions so as to stay calm under pressure; on being in touch with your own emotions so that you understand your own drives and preferences; on being sensitive to the other person's point of view and how that person will respond to any suggestions you might make; and on being able to engage with others in a pleasant, mature, considerate way. In short, what is called for is emotional intelligence of quite a high order.

If you need convincing of what we are saying, just watch any group of people doing a job that is liable to be beyond their collective capability. Look out especially for the first time things don't go according to plan. Very quickly you will start to see those tell-tale signs of agitation: the petulance, the expressed frustration, the snappiness, the hands on hips – what is sometimes called the 'double teapot'. In quick succession follow the making of excuses, assignment of blame, giving up trying and breaking up into factions. Soon the situation is charged with high-octane emotion, and if the situation really deteriorates it isn't long before someone really loses control and stalks off.

Genetically, emotions were laid down first – before the intellect. And that has not changed. Like it or not, emotions drive our behaviour – but not necessarily in any coherent or sensible manner; 'undisciplined squads of emotions' is how TS Eliot put it. The challenge is to decide whether you are going to work with your emotions, or fight them, in an environment that is infinitely more complicated than the one that your ancestors inhabited.

It might simplify matters to think of emotional intelligence as another personality model. Certainly some of the other methods of assessment used at multi-assessment events are intended to throw up observable evidence of many of the personal attributes PQs and EIQs seek to measure. For example, the role-play exercises used as part of the police national selection system are designed to reveal aspects of an individual's EI such as self-regulation, empathy and social skills.

## Emotional intelligence questionnaires – why some selectors use them

Selectors use them for the same reasons they use PQs – because they provide information well worth having that cannot be easily obtained from other sources.

## Emotional intelligence is not the same as ability

Like all questionnaires that seek to tap into behaviour, EIQs are not an objective test – the results, therefore, are suggestive or allusive. Much depends on the skill of the test constructors in giving you options where your preference is actually meaningful. Like PQs, EIQs work on the basis that if you can drill down often enough into some aspect of behaviour a more or less coherent picture will emerge of how a person is likely to behave in certain circumstances or under certain conditions.

## How to prepare for an EIQ – why it is best to tell the truth

Precisely the same rationale applies as for PQs. Your best interests are not served by trying to pretend that you are something you are not. This is even more true of EI where the behaviours are closer to the surface and once triggered are starkly exposed. Swear that you don't have a temper and you will be found out soonest – perhaps under pressure in an interview, at a stressful moment in a role-play activity or when someone disagrees with you in a group decision-making exercise.

## Putting the results of an EIQ into perspective

As with PQs, selectors know that they cannot put too much weight on the results of EIQs because they are only one part of the whole evidential picture. But produce a profile of yourself that you cannot substantiate in an interview and you could be in trouble.

The good news is that you won't get through on the EIQ (if there is one) alone, nor should you fail strictly because of it. So make sure you shine on most of the rest of the assessment centre. The EIQs themselves typically have traps in them to try to catch out 'fakers' although if you are determined to tell lies then you may not be caught out – so much the worse for you. It really is best to reveal yourself sincerely in so far as the questions press you to do so.

## Models of emotional intelligence

There is basically only one model of EI. The elements are self-control, self-awareness, empathy, motivation and social skills. You might find a model using a sixth element, or using variations on these labels, but essentially all those in the field subscribe to the five listed.

In terms of knowing where you stand, we have an exercise for you in **Tables 5.7** to **5.9**. Then you could do the sample questions in **Table 5.10**, after which, if you wanted more, you could go to our book where there are more questions. If you do all that, you will have a pretty good fix on your EI as you go into an assessment centre or multi-assessment event.

The exercise involves pairs of phrases – all you have to do is put a tick (✓) in the box next to the phrase that most accurately describes your typical behaviour and a cross (✗) if it doesn't. If you identify with more phrases on the left than the right in **Table 5.7**, your self-control is more developed than

**Table 5.7** How's your self-control?

| | ✓/✗ | | ✓/✗ |
|---|---|---|---|
| Sleep on it | | Must have it now | |
| Park the problem | | Deal with it head on | |
| Go with the flow | | Force the issue now | |
| Count to 10 | | Blurt it out | |
| Hold something hurtful back | | Say it regardless | |
| Let it go | | Cuss and swear | |
| Let people work out how I am feeling | | Wear my emotions on my sleeve | |
| State my requirements | | Demand what I want | |

**Table 5.8** How's your self-awareness?

| | ✓/✗ | | ✓/✗ |
|---|---|---|---|
| Glass half-full | | Glass half-empty | |
| Respect myself | | I pull myself down | |
| Be true to myself | | Don't properly understand who I am | |
| Understand the impact I have on others | | Surprised by how people react to me | |
| Listen actively to what people say | | Not interested in what others say | |
| Learn from others' experience | | Know everything I need to know | |
| Know what I can and can't do | | Don't know my limitations | |
| See myself warts and all | | Warts, what warts? | |

**Table 5.9** How's your empathy?

| | ✓/✗ | | ✓/✗ |
|---|---|---|---|
| Know how someone else is feeling | | Struggle to work out other people | |
| Believe in 'Do as you would be done by' | | No principles of behaviour guide my life | |
| Feel for someone who fails | | It's their fault: no excuses | |
| There but for the grace of God go I | | Wouldn't let myself get into that situation | |
| Stand or fall together | | You're on your own | |
| Politicians are subject to the same drives as the rest of us | | Don't understand politics | |
| It's fascinating what makes people tick | | People are a closed book | |
| Helping others succeed is a success for me | | Best to get on with your own business | |

not. If it's not either/or (and it probably won't be), see where you lie on an imaginary line between the two poles. The same applies to **Table 5.8** (self-awareness) and **Table 5.9** (empathy). Because so much importance is attached to motivation in the selection of employees, and for places on education and training courses, we have included this aspect of emotional intelligence under a separate heading.

## Some examples of EIQ questions

**Table 5.10** shows some typical EIQ questions. Read each statement and answer according to this key: Always (**A**); Mostly (**M**); Sometimes (**S**); Rarely (**R**); Never (**N**).

**Table 5.10** Examples of EIQ questions

| Statement | A | M | S | R | N |
|---|---|---|---|---|---|
| 1. I'm on a short fuse | | | | | |
| 2. I have to have what I want when I want it | | | | | |
| 3. I worry if I don't sort things out straight away | | | | | |
| 4. I let others know how I am feeling | | | | | |
| 5. I can keep a secret | | | | | |
| 6. I am prepared to be candid about myself | | | | | |
| 7. I have values that guide my everyday behaviour | | | | | |
| 8. I can predict what people will say | | | | | |
| 9. I know if I will like something | | | | | |
| 10. I play to my strengths | | | | | |
| 11. I can put myself in someone else's shoes | | | | | |
| 12. I feel others' pain and joy | | | | | |
| 13. I know what's going to happen next before other people | | | | | |
| 14. I can sense who I will get on with and who I won't | | | | | |
| 15. I don't do anything knowingly to harm other people | | | | | |

Did you recognize what the questions are driving at? The first five are about your self-control, the second five about your self-awareness and the third five about your empathy. How did you get on? Did you know enough about yourself to give an unequivocal answer to each question?

# Motivation

Motivation questionnaires aim to bring to the surface how conditions such as those found in the workplace could affect your motivation. There are no 'right' or 'wrong' answers to these questions, but the expectation is that patterns will emerge from your responses that will tell the recruiters things about you that will be of interest to them. In particular, they will be keen to know if you:

- want to improve your performance and achieve high standards;
- are committed to achieving your goals;
- are prepared to take the initiative and seize your opportunities;
- remain optimistic even in the face of adversity.

## Wanting to improve and to achieve high standards

If you are strong in this aspect of motivation you will have a clear sense of your goals coupled with a determination to set yourself high standards – no easy targets or soft options for you! Given below are some sample questions for you to try. In each case you are asked to choose, from three options, the statement that best captures how you think you would behave in the given situation.

### Question 1

You feel frustrated and irritated by a difficult task you have been asked to undertake. How do you respond?

A Get it over with as quickly as you can but grumble about it to anyone who will listen.

B Keep your frustration to yourself, and get on with it as best you can.

C Take a short break to clear your mind and to devise a plan for tackling the job effectively.

A ☐ B ☐ C ☐

## Question 2

You are working on an important task which you used to find interesting but you have done it so often that you are now bored with it. How do you respond?

A Put it to the bottom of the pile and get on with other more interesting things.
B Get on with it, but giving it only minimal time and attention.
C Think of a fresh way of doing it as quickly and effectively as possible.

A ☐ B ☐ C ☐

## Question 3

Having worked hard to achieve your targets you find that you have exceeded them significantly. How do you respond?

A Enjoy the moment but then sit back and rest on your laurels.
B Enjoy the moment but maintain your effort so that your performance does not slip back.
C Enjoy the moment but build on your success by setting yourself new goals.

A ☐ B ☐ C ☐

## Question 4

You have come up with some ideas for solving a problem but have been told by your colleagues that the ideas have little chance of success. How do you respond?

A Bow to their superior judgement and forget all about it.
B Ignore their advice, trust your own judgement, and get on with it.
C Think about what they have said, modify your ideas, and then take a calculated risk of putting them into practice.

A ☐ B ☐ C ☐

## Question 5

You have been working on a project for a period of time and are experiencing difficulty in judging how well you are doing and how you might do better. How do you respond?

A Just carry on with what you were doing because no one to date has criticized your performance.
B Trust your own judgement and modify your actions accordingly.
C Carry out a self-evaluation, discuss it with someone whose judgement you trust, and modify your actions accordingly.

A ☐ B ☐ C ☐

## Question 6

You are checking through some data with a view to making a decision and realize that some important bits of information are missing. How do you respond?

A Assume that the missing data is unimportant and make a decision on the basis of the information at your disposal.
B Make an informed guess about the missing information and make your decision accordingly.
C Take the trouble to chase up the missing data and only make a decision when all of it is available to you.

A ☐ B ☐ C ☐

## Being committed to achieving your goals

Commitment is widely recognized as a crucial component of motivation – those who lack it rarely achieve to their full potential. On the other hand, there are those who manage to demonstrate, through their commitment and determination to succeed, that they are capable of achieving at a much higher level. In working groups these are people who have strong attachments to their colleagues, and a firm commitment to shared values, and goals. They are the ones who are willing to 'go the extra mile' for the common good. Given below are some sample questions for you to work through following the same procedure as Questions 1–6.

## Question 7

You have been asked to work on a task you dislike intensely. How do you respond?

A Keep putting it off in favour of tasks on which you prefer to work.
B Do it as quickly as you can but with minimum effort.
C Get on with it to the best of your ability giving it as much time and effort as you are able.

A ☐ B ☐ C ☐

## Question 8

You are working on an important task and some colleagues ask you to break off to go for an early evening drink. How do you respond?

A Without any hesitation, turn down their invitation.
B Say that you will join them later if you can even though you have no intention of doing so.
C Thank them for asking and explain why you can't go with them on this occasion.

A ☐ B ☐ C ☐

## Question 9

You are faced with a long and difficult task, which requires hard work and painstaking attention to detail if success is to be achieved. Someone suggests a quick and easy way of doing it. How do you respond?

A Take up the suggestion immediately and get the job done as quickly as you can.
B Ignore the advice and stick to the tried and true method of doing the job irrespective of how long it takes.
C Give careful consideration to the suggestions made, but reject anything which might jeopardize the standard of your work.

A☐ B☐ C☐

## Question 10

You have been asked to take on an extra responsibility which you know is important to your team, but you think that you will find the new role to be too demanding. How do you respond?

A Turn down the request on the grounds that you have more than enough to do already.
B Agree to take it on, but with no intention of giving it priority over your existing commitments.
C Say that despite the hard work the extra responsibility will entail, you are prepared to take it on.

A☐ B☐ C☐

## Question 11

The team of which you are a member has been successful even though your part in its achievements has been minor. How do you respond?

A Decline to join in the celebrations on the grounds that you had little to do with the team's success.
B Congratulate your colleagues and then get on with what you were doing leaving them to celebrate their achievement.
C Show your pleasure at the team's achievements and pride in your own contribution, however minor.

A ☐ B ☐ C ☐

## Question 12

You have been working very hard over a period of months in an attempt to improve your performance, but with little evidence to date that you are succeeding. How do you respond?

A Reduce your efforts on the grounds that you can perform at a level which satisfies other people without having to try so hard.
B Keep going in the belief that you are right to set yourself high goals and that you will achieve them in due course.
C Reaffirm your commitment to achieving your goals, but move to overhaul the methods you are using to achieve them.

A ☐ B ☐ C ☐

## Taking the initiative and seizing opportunities

If you have strengths in this aspect of motivation you are generally more adept than other people at recognizing opportunities in the first place, as well as appreciating their significance.

You are also prepared to persist when others are ready to give up. Thus, when faced with established working practices and rules and regulations which are preventing you from getting on with the job in hand, you and others like you are skilled at devising and implementing creative ways of getting round them. Given below are some more sample questions – work through, following the same procedure as before.

## Question 13

A problem has come to light in something your team is working on, and you think you can help to resolve it. How do you respond?

A Wait to be asked if you have any ideas to offer for solving the problem.
B Put forward your ideas before anyone else has a chance to get in ahead of you.
C Set out your ideas with confidence and ask the team to help you to implement them.

A ☐ B ☐ C ☐

## Question 14

You are a member of a group in which no one but no one will volunteer to take on an important task. You are confident that you could do it well. How do you respond?

A Do nothing – modestly wait to be asked.
B Don't hesitate – volunteer to do the job without consulting anyone.
C Let it be known that you would be willing to take on the task, but that you will need their support.

A ☐ B ☐ C ☐

## Question 15

A vacancy has occurred for a job, which would require you to take on extra work and responsibility. How do you respond?

A Decide not to apply on the grounds that you can do without the hassle.
B Wait to see if someone who is more experienced or better qualified than you submits an application.
C Show that you have confidence in your own ability by submitting an application for the job.

A ☐ B ☐ C ☐

## Question 16

A high-profile working party is being set up to investigate ways of tackling a certain problem. You have not been asked to join, but understand that volunteers may be considered. How do you respond?

A Don't volunteer on the grounds that if you haven't been asked to join already someone must think that you are not really cut out for it.
B Let it be known that if no one else volunteers you will be willing to do so.
C Put your name forward and say that you are confident in your ability to make a difference.

A ☐ B ☐ C ☐

## Question 17

You can see that a crisis is developing and no one present seems willing to take control of the situation. How do you respond?

A Mind your own business – you don't want to get the blame if something goes seriously wrong.
B Put forward as quickly as you can the name of someone who is capable of taking control of the situation.
C Take the initiative by assuming control of the situation until the necessary support arrives.

A ☐ B ☐ C ☐

## Question 18

You have been asked if you would be willing to attend an event as back-up to the main team even though the chances are that you will not be called upon to do anything. How do you respond?

A Turn down the invitation on the grounds that your time would be better spent doing something more productive.
B Accept the invitation but let it be known that you would rather be doing something else.
C Accept the invitation as a chance to be involved and to learn from what will be a new experience.

A ☐ B ☐ C ☐

## Being optimistic even in the face of adversity

If you are strong in this aspect of motivation you will have the ability to continue to work towards achieving your goals in the face of difficulties and unexpected setbacks. At times like these your approach will be optimistic – adopting the advice expressed in the words of the song '*accentuate the positive, eliminate the negative*'. Consequently, you have a tendency to see failure to achieve your goals as being a consequence of circumstances beyond your control rather than as a personal weakness. Given below is a final set of sample questions – work through them in the same way as you did previously.

## Question 19

Some unexpected bad news has left you and your colleagues feeling rather anxious and depressed about future prospects. How do you respond?

A Allow yourself to be drawn into the general mood of pessimism.
B Suggest that you all go out for the evening and put your troubles to one side.
C Do your best to stay cheerful and concentrate your thoughts on trying to find ways of turning the situation to your advantage.

A ☐ B ☐ C ☐

## Question 20

You have been given some negative feedback on your performance, which you were not expecting. How do you respond?

A Flatly refuse to accept the evidence on which the feedback is based.
B Listen to the criticisms without comment, but inwardly reject them.
C Listen carefully to the feedback and consider ways in which you might use it alongside your self-evaluation to improve your performance.

A ☐ B ☐ C ☐

## Question 21

Despite your best efforts you are persistently failing to meet the performance targets you have set for yourself. How do you respond?

A Refuse to give up and resolve to try harder in future.
B Revise your performance targets downwards to a level that you know you can sustain.
C Stick to your performance targets, but re-examine the ways in which you are seeking to achieve them; if necessary, by increasing your efforts.

A ☐ B ☐ C ☐

## Question 22

Without warning you have been asked to change the role in the team you are familiar with for one that will be new to you. How do you respond?

A Turn it down on the grounds that it is unfair to expect you to take on new responsibilities at short notice.
B Agree to do the job for a trial period but only if certain conditions are met.
C Discuss what the new role would entail then, after due consideration, back your own ability to respond to the challenge by accepting the job.

A ☐ B ☐ C ☐

## Question 23

You are working to a strict deadline on an important project when you run into an unexpected problem. How do you respond?

A Keep quiet about it and settle for doing the best that you can, cutting corners if necessary.
B Ask for extra time to complete the work to your satisfaction.
C Do what it takes to complete the project on time to the highest possible standard given the circumstances.

A ☐ B ☐ C ☐

## Question 24

You have just been told that a job interview was unsuccessful even though you appeared to be the best-qualified candidate. How do you respond?

A Pretend that you under-performed in the interview because you did not really want the job.
B Blame yourself for not having done sufficient preparation for the interview.
C Say that you thought that you had a good interview, but that you must have come up against somebody who happened to perform better than you did on the day.

A ☐ B ☐ C ☐

Once you have answered all of the questions, review your responses to see if any overall trends emerge, which tell you about your own patterns of behaviour with regard to motivation.

## Summary

In the course of this chapter we have:

- explained why selectors choose to use personality questionnaires and inventories (these terms were treated as interchangeable);
- acquainted you with the rationale underpinning the design of personality questionnaires (PQs);
- introduced you to the most commonly used models of personality;
- advised you on how to present yourself through PQs where we underscored the importance of developing an informal working model of your own personality;
- given you opportunities to work through some examples of the most commonly used questionnaires;
- finally, and most importantly, offered you constructive suggestions on how to prepare for PQs.

We then repeated the exercise for emotional intelligence and motivation. However, whilst it is most likely that you will be given a PQ, you still need to prepare for all three types of questionnaire.

6

# How to succeed at panel interviews

The **aim** of this chapter is to explain: why interviews are so commonly used in the selection process; how panel interviews differ from one-to-one interviews; how to prepare for a panel interview; and how to cope with the challenges once an interview starts. The general assumption is that you are applying from outside (whether for a job, a place on a training programme or a place on a course of study) and that the interview will occur during an assessment centre or multi-assessment event. However, if you are an internal applicant much of the advice offered here is equally applicable.

## Why interviews are used in the selection process

Interviews are widely used in the selection process because they provide those making the selection with the security of having seen all of the candidates in person. For you the candidate they present you with an opportunity to put your case to the assessors, to seek answers to your questions, and to make some judgements about whether or not you really want the job or the place on the training course that is on offer. The fact is that people have come to expect an interview as part of the selection process – so much so that many applicants would be disappointed indeed if they didn't get one. That is as true for internal as it is for external candidates. There is this deep-seated conviction that if only you can get in front of the interviewers you will at least have a chance of making a convincing case for why they should accept you.

As a candidate, it is important not to forget that interviews are a two-way process – the recruiters should be trying to 'sell' themselves to you every bit as much as you are trying to 'sell' yourself to them. The last thing they want is for you to reject them because you formed a negative impression of their organization or institution during the interview. Indeed, you may well have formed such an impression from the assessment centre as a whole, but the interview is where you will sense it most strongly. Because of this, interviews serve an important public relations function as part of the overall selection process.

## Panel interviews

The whole point about an assessment centre or multi-assessment event is to make a better job of evaluating candidates than it is possible to do in a one-to-one interview – a method on which selectors have depended for far too long. The argument runs as follows. By involving more than one interviewer, it is possible to arrive at decisions that are fair to all the candidates, and are more reliable. That said, if the individual members of a panel tend to share the same attitudes, opinions and biases, their decisions are likely to converge very quickly. So, while assessments made by second interviews conducted by means of a panel will be more reliable than one-to-one interviews, the evidence they provide always needs to be considered alongside that obtained by other methods.

## Number of interviewers

The most off-putting aspect of a panel interview from a candidate's point of view is the number of interviewers asking questions. In general, three interviewers seem to present no problem, but any number greater than that starts to become troublesome, especially if some panel members are seated at the periphery of your vision. In these circumstances it is easy for you to feel exposed and vulnerable – even intimidated. Unfortunately, that is how some selectors, hopefully a minority, may want you to feel during the interview – they appear to see it as an essential part of the test – to see if the candidates can deal with pressure in the interview, on the assumption that they will be able to transfer that ability to the workplace. Hopefully, you should not have to cope with interview practice derived from that philosophy at an assessment centre you attend. If an organization or institution has gone to the trouble and expense of setting up an assessment centre it is most unlikely that they will engage in, or sanction the use of, any intimidatory tactics – unless they are part of an agreed, premeditated strategy designed to reveal how all of the candidates cope with particular kinds of pressure in certain work- or study-related contexts.

As far as the number of panel members is concerned, you really shouldn't let that worry you – in general the more interviewers there are, the better your chances, simply because you increase the probability that you will appeal to one or two interviewers who may then take up your cause when the opportunity arises for them to do so. Above all, you should remember that you have succeeded in getting as far as the interview stage in the overall selection process – you have 'your story' to tell, and now is your chance to do so. Even if one of the panel members doesn't approve of what you say or how you say it, all is not lost. In any case, the panels you are likely to encounter at assessment centres will probably be on the small side because the number of assessors who can be assigned to any one activity is limited. Indeed, you may have to face only two interviewers, one of whom takes notes and hardly asks any questions.

## Note taking

In a panel interview you will see more note taking than you are accustomed to seeing in a one-to-one interview where the interviewer is usually too hard pressed to scribble anything meaningful down. That marks an obvious difference from a panel situation where there are always people free to take notes. In fact, someone may well have been delegated to do the job of taking notes on behalf of the rest, but that will not stop others taking notes if they wish to do so.

Seeing people taking notes is something you have to get used to at an assessment centre or multi-assessment event. Just regard it as an essential part of the process, whether it is during a group exercise, a role-play or an interview. Like the asking of questions or an invitation to you to ask a question, note taking is an integral, routine part of the evidence-gathering procedure and therefore of arriving at a decision that can be defended if needs be. Forget about how much or how little note taking is going on or whether a burst of activity on the part of the panel members is related to anything you have just said – or omitted to say. Unless there is someone there taking verbatim notes, and you will quickly realize who that person is, the amount and frequency of note taking is not driven in any direct way by anything you are doing or saying. Interviewers are obliged to take notes, increasingly for legal reasons, eg for use in the case of a disputed decision that has come before an industrial tribunal. The main reason though concerns human frailty, ie interviewers don't want to have to rely on their memories when it comes to collating evidence about you and the other candidates. As the old saying goes – 'Better a short pencil than a long memory'.

## Observers

Panels can contain observers as well as active interviewers. If one or more of these are present, you should be informed about who they are and why they are present. One of the authors was once interviewed for a post where over twenty people were sitting round a large table. As it turned out, only three asked questions. Such an occurrence is most unlikely to happen to you – the people present as observers in the case cited above being there to represent all sorts of vested interests. Any assessment centre or multi-assessment event you are invited to attend will almost certainly be different – it is unlikely that there will be sufficient resources to afford any over-staffing. If you are troubled by any of the observers who happen to be present, the best advice we can give is to try to put them out of your mind. After all, it may be that the reason they are there has nothing to do with you; they could, for example, be monitoring the way the interview is being conducted, so as to provide feedback on the panel's performance. So, concentrate your attention on the 'sharp end' of the interview, which means the people asking the questions.

## Dividing up the labour

Panel interviewers have the luxury of dividing up the task between them. They will usually do this before the event, ie they will each agree to take responsibility for a particular aspect of the interview. So you might find that the interview structure consists of one person asking you questions around an area of competence, another probing into some aspect of your CV such as your previous work experience, and another following up on any matters that have arisen from the results of the psychometric tests and personality inventories you have completed.

## Rapport

Good interviewers will immediately try to establish a rapport with you. This is more difficult to do in a panel interview – both for them and for you. Naturally, it takes time for each interviewer to establish a relationship with the candidate and if they are not careful they will achieve little else in the time available. So, for their part, they have to strike a balance between establishing rapport with you and pressing ahead with asking questions aimed at obtaining the evidence on which to make judgements about you. From your point of view, you need to remember that, whilst prime responsibility rests with the panel members to establish rapport with you, the empathy on which that is based is a two-way process. So, you should try to: be sensitive to the efforts individual interviewers are making to build rapport with you; and do your best to respond positively to those attempts. The examples given below should help you to interpret correctly any efforts the interviewers are making to establish such a rapport with you.

## Icebreakers

In the event, your interview panel may consist of just two people – in which case there is a good chance that a degree of rapport will be established quite quickly. The process usually starts with a question intended to 'break the ice'. It might be something as mundane as 'Did you have a good journey in?' or 'Is it still raining outside?', or one of the interviewers might pick up on some hobby or achievement spotted in your application form or CV – 'I see you like rock climbing. I used to. Have you ever tried the North Face of the Eiger?' If something like this happens to you, be grateful for it, but don't overreact in response. For example, you might simply say: 'I hear it can be very tricky in winter', and leave it at that.

One of the authors was once interviewing a person with a background in marketing. Her CV showed that she had been responsible for marketing a certain soft drink. When, at the start of the interview, he told her that he and his family liked that drink – couldn't get enough of it – she relaxed visibly and said: 'Let me send you a case. Which do you prefer, the guava or the mango?' Needless to say, the promised case never materialized, but that short interaction succeeded in breaking the ice for her and the interviewers.

## Non-verbal communication

Once the interview has started, look out for signs that the interviewers are interested and are giving you their full attention. These signs will usually be found in the so-called 'body language' of the interviewers. Look out for nodding of the head, smiling and looking intently at you (but not staring). Then there are the signs that they are not giving you their full attention. These include fidgeting with their pens, looking at their notes instead of you, and yawning. Yawning is the worst, especially when it is half-concealed behind a raised hand (as if you don't know what they are doing behind there). But don't allow yourself to be put off. However much you might want to comment on what they are doing, hold your tongue and press on with what you are saying. Hopefully, you will not encounter behaviour of this kind at an assessment centre or multi-assessment event – the professionalism and expertise of those concerned should ensure that it does not happen. In any case, there is always a good chance that a panel member, through her/his body language, will give you some form of encouragement. What though if no one is responding positively to what you are saying? The chances are that you are in fact struggling to make an impact on your audience. In that case it is up to you to make an effort to improve matters.

## Advance preparation

Experience suggests that it is to your advantage to do some preparation in advance for your interview. If you do not already belong to the organization or institution, try to find out about:

- just exactly what it is that the organization or institution does;
- what it produces or what services it provides;
- its origins and history;
- how it is structured and managed – its organization chart is a good starting point;
- the type and number of employees/trainees/students;
- current initiatives and new developments;
- the personnel who lead and manage the organization or institution;
- the nature of any recent press coverage it has received.

You should be able to obtain this kind of information from the relevant website or media sources.

Having done the preliminary 'legwork' of this kind, think about what questions you may be asked in the interview and begin to prepare some answers. That should help to 'take the sting out' of some of the questions, which might otherwise surprise you. A few questions on which you might do preparatory work are listed in the box below. Some of these questions are intended to probe quite deeply, so you might want to involve someone to help you to bring some of the answers to the surface – ideally that person will be someone who knows you well and whose judgement you trust.

You should also be prepared to answer questions about your health, about more technical questions related to your qualifications, research or current job, and about any interests you have mentioned on your CV, application form or letter. So, when compiling your CV, filling in an application form or writing your covering letter, do bear in mind that anything you say about yourself might become the subject of some searching

## Preparing in advance: some interview questions to think about

- Why have you applied for this job/training opportunity/course of study?
- Why did you choose the course you did at college/university?
- Which aspects of the course did you find most enjoyable, least enjoyable, most difficult and least difficult and for what reasons?
- What are you looking for in this opening?
- What do you regard as your personal strengths?
- In terms of your personal profile, which areas of competence do you think you need to improve?
- When you have a deadline to meet, what do you do to ensure that you meet it?
- When you have had to choose a partner or team members to work with on a project, how did you go about making that choice?
- What do you think makes for a good team or working group?
- Why would others want to have you on their team or working group?
- What would you do if you found that a member of your team was not pulling her or his weight?
- Tell me about a time when something has not gone well for you. What did you do to overcome this? What would you do differently next time?
- How do you see this opportunity fitting into your longer-term career path?
- What else or where else have you applied for, and how are your applications progressing?
- Why do you want a change? (Try not to be overly critical about your current employer/education institution/placement – you could end up giving a preview of how well you complain and that would go down like the proverbial 'lead balloon'.)
- What sort of things put you under pressure? Give an example and explain how you cope.
- What would your colleagues/fellow students say about you?
- Tell me about a presentation you have done. How did you prepare for it? What went well? What went badly?
- What do you know about us? Have we been in the news recentiy? (The answer might just be 'No' but you need to know.)

questions in an interview. Talking of searching questions, the following box gives some more for you to think about. Again, the advice would be to work through the questions, and your answers to them, with a confidant.

> **Advance preparation: some tougher interview questions to think about**
>
> - Why are you looking to move into a new job?
> - What do you want from your new position?
> - What could you do better?
> - What type of work environment are you most suited to?
> - What type of colleague are you?
> - What plans do you have for the future – both medium- and longer-term?
> - Why do you feel you are suited to this vacancy?
> - Why should we select you as opposed to other candidates?

## Common failings at interviews

A survey by the recruitment organization Office Angels pinpointed three key areas where interviewees consistently fail to impress. They were: inappropriate dress (30 per cent); arrogance (27 per cent); and monosyllabic responses (25 per cent). Indeed, candidates in general seem to be getting the simplest things wrong; almost half (48 per cent) of the employers claimed that they had had people arrive late for interviews without even offering an apology – an issue we addressed in **Chapter 1** under the heading 'Punctuality' along with the matter of 'Dress codes'.

Now an applicant being late is certainly irritating from the point of view of an interview panel, but being arrogant is almost certainly a quicker way to an early exit – it is funny how the two often go together.

## Arrogance

Arrogance is behaviour on the part of individuals that typically attracts the following descriptors: 'cocky', 'pushy', 'self-important', 'uppity', 'self-centred' and 'on her (or his) own agenda'. Basically, what selectors don't like is a lack of humility – an attitude that seems to be saying 'I know it all' or, as we say, 'I've got attitude'. Here are some examples we have come across in our time as interviewers:

- 'I can think quickly on my feet – I don't need to do any advance preparation.'
- 'Unlike some people, I can just look at a problem and know immediately how to tackle it.'
- 'I get on well enough with other people – it's their problem if they can't get on with me.'
- 'I have shown before that I can lead a group – why should this group be any different?'
- 'You don't need to be competent with figures. We have calculators and computers to do that.'
- 'I know who I am and I like it.'

Can we suggest that you read through these assertions again? If you know or suspect that you convey or are liable to convey impressions of this kind to others, you would be well advised to reflect on your behaviour and to modify it accordingly. What you must beware of is overcompensating because if you do that you will no longer be true to yourself – something that will be readily apparent to an experienced interview panel. Don't confuse confidence with overconfidence.

The situation is undoubtedly complicated by the fact that interviewers sometimes voice a preference for candidates who display what they refer to as 'personality' or 'charisma' – indeed they have been known to say that they prefer them to 'dull clones'. The solution for you is to be confident, but be aware that there is a thin line between presenting an image of yourself that can be admired and presenting one that can be criticized. What selectors often call 'arrogance' is in fact a collection of observable behaviours that is perhaps best described as 'inappropriate' in a particular context. Trying to 'show off' in front of an interview panel is doomed to failure. It is far more profitable to make the panel aware that you are socially tuned in and that you can be tactful and sensitive when interacting with people – above all your interviewers. The interview is a good place for you to display those personal attributes associated with self-control (you will need it if you are provoked), self-awareness (who is this 'I' they are trying to find out about?), empathy (rapport again) and social skills. These are the building blocks of emotional intelligence, a quality increasingly prized by recruiters. You will have studied what we had to say about emotional intelligence in **Chapter 5**.

## Monosyllabic answers

You can be late and arrogant but still have something to say. You can be punctual and modest and have nothing to say. Interviewers really do not care for candidates who are over-economical with their use of words. You must be prepared to open up and talk – after all that is the whole point of having an interview. This is your 'day in court', as it were. Why would you want to keep quiet? Had the selectors simply wanted to hear 'Yes' and 'No' answers they would have sent you a questionnaire to complete online instead of going to the expense of inviting you to an interview as part of a wider programme of exercises at an assessment centre. No matter how well you perform on the other assessment exercises you cannot afford to underachieve at the interview stage of the proceedings so get those lips moving. Again, if you think you have a tendency to shyness and might just clam up, do some work beforehand on loosening yourself up, again with a trusted friend or relative. Simply ask them to pitch some of the questions in the boxes.

## The interview

Now we have reached the interview itself and you are standing at the threshold. So, gather yourself up and enter the room confidently – don't just sidle into the presence of your interviewers as if you would prefer to do so without being noticed. When greeting the panel, look them in the eyes and smile. If the panel chairperson offers to shake your hand, do so and then repeat the process with the other members of the interview panel. That is simply you being confidently proactive and demonstrating your social skills. Once you are seated and the interview is under way, communicate to your interrogators that you are giving them your full attention. The best way to do this is by means of eye contact with your interviewers and by listening attentively to what they have to say. Even though you may not feel exactly that way, try to communicate to them that you are alert and self-confident. Remember, don't slouch and don't lose eye contact by gazing at the wall or out of the window. If you get the opportunity to do so, ask relevant questions. In short, try to behave as if the interview has presented you with the chance you have been looking for to move forwards in your career, and that you are keen to avail yourself of the opportunity – and have the motivation necessary to succeed. Without going over the top and becoming overconfident, don't be afraid to 'sell' yourself. After all, you may need what the selectors have to offer more than the organization or institution they represent needs you!

To sum up, in order to perform effectively in the panel interview, you need to do the following:

- Communicate that you are alert and are giving the proceedings your full attention.
- Listen to the questions – and answer them as fully and honestly as you can.
- Take each point in turn and ask for clarification if necessary.
- If you don't know the answer to a question, say so.
- Don't give one-word answers, such as 'Yes' and 'No': develop your responses, eg 'Yes. I would be happy to take on the additional responsibility if given an opportunity to do so.'
- Use 'I' not 'we', unless you are talking about working with others in a team.

When it is your turn to ask questions, use it as an opportunity to: show what you know about the organization or institution; and clarify any areas of uncertainty about the job, training opportunity or course of study. There is no harm in taking a list of questions in with you – but don't overdo the questions and don't, when the chairperson wants to bring matters to a conclusion, sign off by saying, 'Er, yes, I think that's all.' It sounds weak and indecisive and leaves you psychologically somewhat up in the air. If you have questions, make them crisp and to the point and make sure that they elicit what you are after – which is as much as you need to know about the opening for which you are being interviewed.

## Types of questions interviewers ask

Since the primary objective of the interview is to obtain evidence from you, it follows that you should do most of the talking. Specifically, the interview panel should aim to have you talking approximately 70–80 per cent of the time. The knack of bringing that off lies in the type of questions they ask and the way they respond to what you have to say.

## Open questions

Open questions enable you to provide facts and information, describe events and express your feelings or opinions. In short, they should get you talking. Examples would be: 'Tell me about the duties in your present job' and 'How do you deal with an irate member of the public?' To open questions such as these you will find it very difficult – unless you restrict yourself to monosyllabic answers – to avoid being drawn into a stream of talk that is more or less informative according to how well you do it. Fortunately, one of the saving graces of questions of this kind is that the topics on which they are based are fairly predictable, in which case you should be well prepared for them. That should enable you to seize the initiative by imposing a structure on your answer, which is to your advantage. For example, in response to the first question given above you might begin by saying 'According to my current job description I have four main areas of responsibility... But in reality I find most of my time is taken up with...'

## Closed questions

Closed questions are very different – you can answer 'Yes' or 'No', and in both cases the answer would be a sufficient reply. You can see why this is the case if you think about how you might answer these closed questions: 'Did you enjoy your last job?' and 'Did you get on well with your supervisor?'

Interviewers find that closed questions are useful for checking their understanding of your answers or specific pieces of information you have volunteered. However, they are not good for getting you to open up and talk – and in so doing providing the range and depth of evidence they are seeking to acquire. If interviewers are asking you a lot of closed questions they are not doing their job: they might as well have handed you a questionnaire. If it does happen that you are being asked one closed question after another and you feel you are not doing yourself justice you can always expand on your answer without being asked to do so. What you must do though is to proceed tentatively, eg by saying 'I would like to develop that point further if I may' or by asking 'Before I answer the question directly would it be helpful if I said something first about the situation in which I was working?' The interviewers can only say 'No' but will in all likelihood say 'Yes'. Note that taking this last approach shows that you are trying to be sensitive to the panel's needs.

## Multi-headed questions

Multi-headed questions occur when two or more questions are bundled up into one over-wordy question. Political commentators, who are anxious to get their questions asked, are always doing it at news conferences. However, there is really no need for this to happen in a panel interview – except it will. Like this one: 'Why exactly have you applied for this job/course, where do you see yourself in five years' time and why have you decided on a change of direction at the present time?' If you are asked a multi-headed question of this kind, the temptation is to focus on the question you would prefer to answer and to ignore those that you consider to be more awkward – or that might reveal a weakness to the interviewers. It will not have escaped your notice that experienced politicians are very adept at doing this! Of course it is possible to respond in such a way as to address all of the questions (if you can remember them). For example, in response to the multi-header asked above you might begin by saying 'The reasons why I am considering a change of direction are related to the factors that led to my applying for this post/course, and in turn that is related to where I would like to be in five years' time.' Having set up your response in that way you can then proceed to identify those aspects of, for example, the job being offered, including any personal development and career progression opportunities that may have been promised.

## Leading questions

In a leading question the answer the interviewer expects to hear is given away in the question itself. This usually occurs where the interviewer prefaces the question with some information from either the job description or the person specification. For example: 'In this job you have to lick a lot of stamps. How do you feel about licking stamps?'; or 'We are looking for somebody who can work to deadlines. How well do you work to deadlines?' If you are lucky enough to get questions like these, make the most of them – but on no account use it as an opportunity to poke fun at the interviewers: 'Licking stamps – I love it. I can never get enough of it. I would count it a poor day if I did not lick some stamps'; and 'Deadlines – they're a doddle. I eat deadlines. If I didn't have deadlines, I couldn't get out of bed in the morning.' Of course, you won't get such questions, but you take the point.

## Hypothetical questions

With a hypothetical question the interviewer describes a situation to you and asks you what you would do in the circumstances. Interviewers tend to be fond of such questions because they project you into possibly uncharted waters and are therefore more of a challenge, but they really ought to be asking you how you handled similar situations in the past, rather than trying to see how you might handle a situation in the future. So, rather than asking 'How would you deal with an irate customer if you were faced with one?', they should ask: 'Can you give me an example of when you had to deal with an irate member of the public?' If you should be asked a hypothetical question you will know what to say: something along the lines of 'I would remain calm, write down the details and promise to contact a senior colleague immediately.'

## Multiple-choice questions

This is the oral equivalent of a multiple-choice item in a psychometric test. It is the one where the interviewer asks a question and provides the candidate with a number of answers to select from. For example: 'How did you find out about this job? Was it through the job centre, your careers teacher, an advertisement, a friend who already works for the company, or what?' Here the interviewer is obviously doing your work for you – so let him or her. Quite often the first part of the question (in this case, 'How did you find out about this job?') is good enough on its own – and is in fact the nub of the question. As always, it is essential to listen carefully to what the questioner is saying, and to answer accordingly.

## Turning weaknesses into strengths

There is something high-risk about trying to turn weaknesses into strengths. If you attempt it, proceed with care. There are people who think that this is one way of succeeding in an interview – but don't be too sure. You might think you are being very clever in talking about one of your weaknesses in such a way that it comes over as being one of your strengths, but any competent panel of interviewers will quickly see through what you are trying to do. 'What are your weaknesses?' you are asked, and you reply along the lines, 'I ask too much of myself.' Anything else? 'I ask too much of others so when they fail to deliver I get disappointed. I am afraid that my standards are just too high for some people.' You may think you have finessed the question beautifully by stressing your virtues, but the interviewers are all too likely to have made a note to the effect that you are 'Unwilling to reveal and discuss weaknesses'.

## Systematic interviewing based on competencies

At an assessment centre or multi-assessment event there is every chance that your interview will be conducted systematically around statements of competence judged to be relevant to the job, training opportunity or course of study for which you have applied. Take a competency like 'achievement drive', which will be deemed relevant for many occupations, as it should be. An example of a systematic sequence of questions around this competency would be: 'In the application form, you described a situation where you achieved something difficult. Tell me more', followed by: 'Why did you pursue this particular objective?', 'What setbacks did you encounter?', 'How did you overcome them?', 'Was anyone else involved?', 'How did you motivate them to work with you?' and 'What was the outcome?' You will see from this example that the interviewers are 'funnelling down', as the jargon has it (you might say 'drilling down' or 'bottoming out'), in order to satisfy their curiosity about the person's achievement drive.

The interviewers might ask a similar sequence of questions in relation to a second area of competence if more evidence is required. They could also inject additional questions, like 'Could you describe a time when you have tried to accomplish something, but failed?' followed by 'How did the situation arise?', 'What did you learn from this experience?' and 'How have you put what you learnt into practice?' Try to familiarize yourself with this style of questioning because you are likely to encounter it at some point.

Competence-based interviewing is designed to provide specific evidence of what you have done in the past. By asking about real events and marking your answers against behavioural indicators, skilled interviewers are able to get a firm fix on the nature of your achievement drive or whichever area of competence is the focus of their attention.

## Other ways of structuring the interview

Don't expect that areas of competence will always be used as a basis for structuring the interview. The panel may decide instead to work through your CV in chronological order. If that happens, you can expect them to explore such matters as: your experiences, reasons for job or other changes, significant decisions you have made, and your personal aspirations. Although the interview is structured in this way, the panel will still have a clear set of criteria (possibly based on areas of competence) against which to evaluate the information they gleaned from you.

## Killer questions

If you feel that the interview is going well don't allow yourself to be lulled into a false sense of security. That is just the time when one of the interviewers might decide to break up what has become an all-too-comfortable chat and catch you unawares with an unexpected question – 'Why should I offer the chance to you rather than to one of the other candidates?' Wham, how did you like that? It's a so-called 'killer question'. Expect to receive them – in a recent survey by Office Angels of over 500 UK employers, 75 per cent of employers admitted that they ask a 'killer question'. If you are lucky it will just be one. Why ask them at all? Employers are apt to say that killer questions are not deliberately designed to catch people out but rather to encourage those they are interviewing to think on their feet. With over two-thirds (68 per cent) of interviewers claiming candidates could be better prepared and show greater enthusiasm, answering these questions confidently, they say, could mean the difference between success and failure. You didn't think the other one was much of a killer question? Well, how about these? 'What was the question you didn't want us to ask you?', 'Would you ever lie in the interests of your career?', 'Name five current members of the Cabinet' and 'Name three things to remember you by.' If you get asked the last question, try 'Faith, hope and charity' – it might just stick.

You might decide that you do not want anything further to do with an organization that sanctions such a style of questioning (assuming it has been sanctioned, which you won't know anyway). It is always your prerogative to back out – at an assessment centre it is not just the assessors who are entitled to make choices. What we would say is that you are less likely to encounter so-called 'killer questions' at an assessment centre or multi-assessment event. The chances are that the interviewers will have organized themselves properly, and having done that will systematically ask you questions derived from an interview schedule, whether structured by competence or by some other variables.

## Summary

To summarize the advice you have been given in this chapter, here is a final checklist of things we recommend that you do – and some things we suggest you avoid doing:

- Before your interview, do plenty of research on the organization or institution.
- Make a note of your interviewers' names and positions – potentially one of them could be your new boss/course leader.
- Arrive ahead of time.
- Dress smartly and remember to smile – this instantly creates a good impression.
- Be yourself within reason – but if 'yourself' is full of 'attitude', have a care.
- Listen carefully to the questions and answer them as fully and honestly as you can.
- Make good, steady eye contact with your interviewers.

- Be self-confident and alert.
- Make sure you find out as much as you need to about what is on offer.
- Don't ask too many questions, but ask some questions.
- If you can, avoid giving 'Yes' and 'No' as answers – try to elaborate wherever possible.
- Don't be afraid to prepare a list of questions in advance of your interview.
- Don't gabble – it is better to speak slowly and clearly.

Finally, we have assumed throughout that there is some specific opening for which you have applied. Sometimes with assessment centres and multi-assessment events this is not necessarily the case – the organization may simply be taking a look at you with regard to some possible future advancement. Notwithstanding the distinction, everything we have said in this chapter applies to assessment situations where your potential is being evaluated. What it means is that when asking questions about your future prospects and aspirations you will have to cast the net more widely than if you were applying for a specific opening.

7

# In-tray/in-box, case study and role-play exercises

The **aims** of this chapter are: to familiarize you with in-tray/in-box, case study and role-play exercises, which you might encounter at an assessment centre or a multi-assessment event; and offering advice that will help you to prepare for them.

## In-tray/in-box exercises

The basic idea behind this type of assessment exercise is to confront you with a set of material typical of that which might be found in someone's in-tray. You then have a certain amount of time to study the contents of that in-tray, work out how you would deal with each item and action your decisions (eg by writing a reply to a letter or calculating an estimate of costs from financial data provided). Assessment is usually done by means of a detailed scoring procedure based on how a candidate deals with each item. In some instances you may be asked to make a choice between several alternatives, and in others the assessment may be augmented by evidence derived from a debriefing interview. Such assessment exercises are useful for the purposes of personnel selection because they:

- are quite realistic and representative of the tasks people routinely encounter in their day-to-day roles in the workplace;
- produce evidence of how candidates behave in response to a range of chosen tasks;
- provide evidence of the extent to which candidates possess the required competencies;
- can be linked to other activities in an assessment centre or multi-assessment event programme such as role-play and group discussion exercises.

Clearly, the issues that arise from the contents of an in-tray, and the competencies the exercise is seeking to address, will vary according to the context (eg you would expect an exercise designed to select someone for an administrative support role to be different from one intended for use with prospective senior managers). Nevertheless, in-tray/in-box exercises typically focus on a range of carefully chosen (and relevant) issues placed in context, such as:

- health and safety;
- maintaining the flow of work;
- dealing with unexpected contingencies;
- the delivery of services;
- interpersonal relationships within the organization;
- external relations (eg dealing with members of the public);
- handling enquiries;
- responding to instructions/requests from senior colleagues.

Whilst in-tray/in-box exercises are an effective means of assessing a candidate's ability to exercise effective situational judgement under the pressure of being assessed, there is a possibility that you may not be asked to do one – a reminder of the importance of checking the details of the timetable of any assessment centre or multi-assessment event to which you are invited.

It is now easy for you to practice for this type of assessment exercise – all you have to do is spend some time conducting an online search. A good place to start your search is university careers services, many of which offer comprehensive advice together with examples you can work through – take a look for example, at Bristol, Edinburgh and Leeds. Employers are a second useful source – the Civil Service web page Fast Stream should get you started. In working through practice materials such as these, you need to be aware of the following:

- At an assessment centre you will have to work within strict time limits, during which you will have to: read each item (there can be as many as 20) as quickly and effectively as you can; make a decision about what action you would recommend in each case; and keep a record of all your decisions and the reasoning behind them.
- The interconnectedness of the contents of the in-tray, which means that any action(s) you recommend for one item will have an impact on the decisions you make in relation to some or all of the others.

## Example of an in-tray/in-box exercise

The example in the box below has been chosen to illustrate these points. Work your way through it and you will grasp the general principles that underpin exercises of this kind and gain an insight into the ways in which they are designed.

### The scenario

You are an employee of Kidsplace, producer and distributor of playthings for children. Coinciding with the recent appointment of a new Managing Director (MD), the company has diversified into collectable cards and figures hoping to capitalize on the commercial success of Pokémon.

For the past six months, sets of cards and figures have been tested in three regions of the UK. While Pokémon was at the height of its success the outlook for these products was good, but the market is volatile and the MD will soon have to take a decision as to whether to venture more deeply into this market or consider alternatives.

Presently, you are a member of a small team within Sales and Marketing. You share a secretary and an assistant with the other staff. Most of your work is to do with supporting existing brands, but from time to time you are asked to help evaluate ideas for new brands. You get involved more than most in this activity. The MD will also be relying on you for help with market data and trends as she considers her strategic options and her investment decisions.

It is 9 am on Monday, 28 July and you have just returned from two weeks' leave to find a full in-tray/in-box. At the forefront of your mind is a meeting you are due to have at 11 am with the rest of the team including your immediate superior. A few items in your in-tray are bound to come up at that meeting, but you don't know for certain which ones they will be – so you need to be prepared for all eventualities.

Your task is:

1. To go through the contents, prioritizing the items in the order you intend to deal with them. A sheet is provided for you to write down the order, starting at the top and working down (the items are numbered). You should also specify the type of action you intend taking, and what the justification for that action is.
2. Once you have established an order, start to work your way through the items in the time available (90 minutes).
3. You should make an effort to work through most, if not all, of the items. If you have to defer making a telephone call, say why, and when you intend to do so.

That then is how this type of exercise is set up. Typically, the opening scenario will be accompanied by the in-tray itself, which will usually consist of 20 or so items for you to work through. These will have been selected to make demands on both your judgement and your time – one of the purposes of the exercise being to see how well you can manage your time, organize your priorities and cope under pressure. It is unlikely, therefore, that you will be able to deal with everything – so it will be up to you to optimize your output. Without reproducing exact items you can expect to find in your tray some or all of the items listed in the following box.

## Contents of the in-tray/in-box

- A letter from a group of concerned parents bemoaning the commercial exploitation of young children – they really mean the parents. Pokémon products, they say, already cost far too much, and now there is the addition of this latest fad. Your job will be to draft a reply for someone senior to sign – or you might ask someone else to do it instead.
- Some items that on the face of it look trivial but actually require some thought and immediate attention – what is known as a 'quick judgement call'. For example, whether to attend the Gdansk Toy Fair next week where your competitors are exhibiting, or a complaint from another department about the shared secretary – is this your business, or the team's, and how should you deal with it?
- One or two items of a social nature that may contain the seeds of conflict with more obviously work-related activities.
- An item with a personal tinge where, again, there may be pressure on your time if you try to keep all or most of 'the balls in the air'.
- An enquiry from the Sales Director – accompanied by a spreadsheet of sales figures and a market research report – as to whether the company should be pushing cards or figures and on what evidence.
- An item suggesting that some internal friction is in the offing. You are expecting help from a colleague (hereafter known as 'Viv') in compiling data for the MD, but is that help going to be forth-

coming? A somewhat airy note from that colleague suggests not and leaves you feeling emotionally uneasy and frankly a bit irate.

- A request from the MD for a meeting next Monday to find out how the report is shaping up. (What report? Help!)
- Bits of disparate data from the publicity and cuttings people that have to be processed and massaged into that report.
- Blank sheets of paper headed 'Memos' and 'Telephone Messages' are provided for your use.

Although the list provided above looks formidable, that may not be all. The designers of assessment centres and multi-assessment events may ordain that at some time or times during the course of the exercise you will be presented with new items. These may be entirely new, or more likely pertaining to items that are already in the tray – and significantly that you have already dealt with earlier in the exercise. Given this eventuality, what do you do then? Well, you press on and, in so doing, try to show the assessors that you are capable of dealing with a multiplicity of things simultaneously – and coping with the unexpected contingencies they have introduced as and when they arise. After all, what they are doing is simply seeking to simulate some of the day-to-day realities of life and work in an organization.

In practice, there would be a set of performance criteria for use in evaluating the quality of your decisions and arriving at an overall assessment for the exercise. For example, you could expect to be assessed on the extent to which your decisions on what should be judged as being of high, medium or low priority coincide with those of a group of expert assessors. That is where you need a sense of reality and expediency. So, remember, when doing this type of exercise, always try to think strategically by seeking to link up as many items as you can, ie kill two (or more) birds with one stone.

# Case study exercises

A case study is a realistic and relevant business problem. Candidates typically are asked to analyse the problem, interpret data, consider alternatives and produce a written report describing their solutions or recommendations. Such case study exercises are useful because they:

- provide a reasonably direct measure of relevant skills;
- are convenient to administer, eg they can be done in groups;
- are easy to interpret because detailed performance indicators can be used;
- are relatively easy to construct and customize.

The competencies that the case study exercise is intended to tap into will have been given names like 'analytical thinking', 'situational judgement', 'planning and organizing' and 'communication' – in fact very similar to those assessed by means of in-tray exercises. Consequently, the assessors will judge your performance using a set of indicators organized around headings such as these. If you are still unsure about how you measure up against the relevant competencies we suggest that you carry out the self-audit given in the **Appendix**. In so doing, you would be well advised to pay particular attention to the following categories:

- oral and written communication skills;
- planning and prioritizing work;
- making decisions;
- problem solving.

## Example of a case study

You can imagine how easily a case study could be developed out of the Kidsplace scenario. What would happen is that you (known as 'Sam') would be furnished with the statistics already in the in-tray/in-box plus other information, some of which has been filtered through a person known as 'Viv'. (You should know that there is friction between you and Viv – but that is the subject of the role-play exercise discussed below.) Your task would then be to use the information provided to prepare a strategic report for the MD.

### The case interview

You should be aware that you could find yourself in a variant of the case study, which is the **case interview**. Instead of doing a write-up of the case you will be placed in an interview format and asked to answer questions about the case. A lead-off question for a case interview structured around the Kidsplace company could be: 'When the MD has to take a decision on whether to venture more deeply into the cards and figures market, what factors will she need to have at the forefront of her mind?' While you will have been supplied with enough data to enable you to make a sensible reply to this question and others that follow, what you will need to remember is that in case interviews there are no 'right answers': interviewers look for problem-solving skills, creativity and the ability to appreciate the way in which one decision is likely to have a knock-on effect on several others. To do well in the case interview (which may not be advertised in advance) you will need to utilize all the skills you brought to bear in the panel interview – and some others besides. In particular, you will need to draw upon your analytical skills and your ability to think on your feet.

## Role-play exercises

These are one-to-one exercises where the candidate is engaged in some form of encounter (eg an interview or meeting) with a person who has been given a thorough briefing about his or her role. An assessor or assessors observe(s) the interactions between the two – video recordings being made in some circumstances for monitoring purposes. The assessor(s) may question the candidate afterwards to find out more about the strategy, direction and outcomes of the interactions.

Role-play exercises of this kind have several advantages when it comes to selecting people at an assessment centre, in particular they:

- allow direct observation of a candidate's interpersonal/social skills;
- are realistic, especially with regard to managerial tasks;
- can be tailored to suit a range of tasks and situations that successful candidates are likely to encounter in the workplace.

The disadvantages are that candidates can feel that they have been put into an artificial situation and that they lack the background knowledge from which to determine how best to respond.

## Use of actors

A development you might well encounter is the use of professional role-players, usually actors, to play roles opposite the candidate. It has been our experience that candidates can have difficulty in coping with the problems that these actors bring to the situation, eg when taking on the role of a dissatisfied customer or an irate work colleague. This of course contributes greatly to the authenticity of the situations which are being simulated, thus increasing the validity of the exercise from an assessment point of view.

## Example of a role-play exercise

Again we return to the Kidsplace company. The best designers of assessment centres or multi-assessment events always try to have a theme, which runs all the way through the programme. This, of course, should be a help to you because it means that you are able to immerse yourself in just one specific context rather than several.

As already indicated, there is friction, perhaps even animosity, between Sam and Viv. You get a sense of it from the in-tray/in-box items, especially the note from Viv. Plainly, you as Sam are expecting a sizeable input from Viv to your report for the MD but it does not look as if you are going to get it. The subject of the role-play therefore, is a 'clear-the-air' meeting (or 'confrontation') with Viv. It will be a one-to-one meeting, with you playing Sam and an actor playing Viv.

## The actor's briefing

The actor will be closely briefed as to how to respond to your behaviour. So to give you an idea, here is an example of the kind of briefing the actor gets. One-to-one role-play exercises demand a high level of skill and preparation on the part of the role-player if they are to be effective. The role-player is there to enable the participant to demonstrate his or her strengths in face-to-face situations. Thus the role-player needs to be sufficiently restrained to present a challenge to the participant, yet not be so obstructive that the participant has no chance to resolve the issues. Furthermore, the role must be played consistently with different participants, to ensure fairness and permit valid comparisons to be made. Specifically, these are the kind of guidelines actors get to encourage them to maintain an objective approach:

- It is important that you give a consistent performance throughout – do not vary the role you are playing (aggressive to one participant, mild to another).
- It is a reactive role. The initiative rests with the participant, and you should react naturally to the comments made. If they annoy you, show your annoyance, but do not go over the top. If they make you feel at ease then respond accordingly.

- Try to let the participant lead except when directed to the contrary by the brief.
- If the participant appears to be struggling then assist by giving appropriate information to keep the discussion moving.
- If the discussion comes to an early resolution then let it end.
- Make sure you can see the time so that you can bring the discussion to a close at the end of 20 minutes (or whatever the time limit is).
- Allow participants to develop arguments by giving the candidate time to think and not interrupting too frequently.
- Certain ploys can be useful to stretch a participant, eg 'I'm surprised to hear you say that. My previous Team Leaders never raised that as an issue.'
- Stay within the intentions of the brief, eg if an answer or a question is not listed in the brief, then make one up from your own experience.
- Maintain the focus detailed in the brief, ie do not stray into new issues.

So you can see that essentially the actor's job is to be reactive to whatever you say. The actor will be given a series of 'buttons' she or he can press depending on what you say and how the interactions with you develop. If you lose your temper with Viv, the actor will be told what to do – trade 'verbal blows' or 'stay cool' according to how you play it. Viv will of course have a defence that you may not know about in advance, especially around other demands on her/his time. Consequently, Viv could confront you with things that will come as a surprise to you, and to which you will have to respond constructively there and then. This is not a black-and-white scenario where you are the person who has been 'wronged' and Viv is the perpetrator – but you can play it like that if you choose and see how far you get.

Remember that at the end of the day you and Viv will have to get on, and you still have to produce a report for the MD. The last thing you want to do is to go to her/him crying foul (although you might have already done so in your in-tray exercise). So, the two of you have to resolve your differences and work out what can be done to best advantage in the time available.

## What to do in role-plays

You will usually get something like 20–30 minutes to prepare. In this kind of one-to-one encounter with its undercurrents of friction or resentment (there are others although this is often the kind you will get), try to:

- Get in role at the outset – don't be half in and half out of your role.
- Take what the other role-player says and does seriously.
- Be civil, not angry and rude, from the start of the encounter – even if the other person's behaviour is impolite towards you.
- Have a plan for bringing the encounter to a satisfactory conclusion – and stick to it as far as you can.
- Plan to extract some agreement (even concessions) from the other person.
- Work out how you are going to close the meeting.
- Have a clear idea of next steps and write them down.
- Be firm, never petulant.

## Practice role-play exercises

Now that you have worked through a typical role-play scenario in detail, here are some additional examples for you to practise on as part of your preparation for the role-play exercises:

- **Example 1.** In your role as a Manager you have to deal with a complaint from an irate shop assistant that two adolescents are creating a nuisance in the shopping centre for which you are responsible.

- **Example 2.** In your role as a Security Officer in a department store you have to deal with a senior citizen who has lost his wallet, which contains his pension book, and who is feeling both angry and distressed.
- **Example 3.** In your role as the Office Manager you have to deal with a complaint from one of your staff (a black woman) that she has been the victim of racial abuse from her supervisor.
- **Example 4.** You are the senior waiter on duty in a restaurant and you have to deal with a complaint from a male customer, who appears to have had rather too much to drink, that the food has been poor and that the service has been shoddy.

## Summary

In this chapter we have: familiarized you with in-tray/in-box, case study and role-play exercises, which you might encounter at an assessment centre or a multi-assessment event; and offered some practical advice to help you to prepare for them.

8

# Rounding off your preparation for an assessment centre

The **aim** of this chapter is to offer you some advice on rounding off your preparation ahead of your attendance at an assessment centre or multi-assessment event. Given the nature of the assessment exercises you are likely to encounter we intend to concentrate on your reading and listening skills. We make no apology for devoting an entire chapter to these important skills.

## Improving your reading skills

At a number of points in this book you have been advised to read the instructions and questions carefully to make sure that you understand them and that you have assimilated all the relevant written information before you start on the exercise. In case there is any doubt about this, just think what reading skills enable you to do:

- Perform to the best of your ability in psychometric tests.
- Supply answers to personality and emotional intelligence questionnaires that are a true reflection of who you are.
- Assimilate the written information you are given in connection with group decision-making, in-tray/in-box and case study exercises.
- Deal appropriately with the situations you encounter in the role-play activities.

In each of these examples, if you fail to recognize the significance of information provided, misread the instructions you have been given or misinterpret what someone says, you cannot hope to give the correct answers or deal appropriately with the problems presented to you in different situations. The pressure of being assessed also comes into the equation – your ability to cope under pressure being part of what the assessors will be trying to establish. Hence, deliberately imposed limits on the amounts of time you are given to read the text in front of you, make decisions and respond according to the instructions. This issue will be particularly potent in the psychometric tests – as you will know from your previous experience of taking tests and examinations. There is always a balance to be struck between reading the text quickly enough to get through it all in the time available and reading it carefully enough to be able to understand it and to extract the relevant information. So the message is: brush up your reading skills if you have any reason to suppose that they are in any way below par. Your success could ultimately depend upon it.

Unfortunately, the problem with reading is that once we have learnt to do it we have a tendency to take it for granted. We seem to think that, like riding a bike, once you have learnt how to do it you no longer have to think about it, as it is something you never forget how to do. In fact, what many people don't realize is that over the years they have developed a wide range of reading skills, which they deploy without ever having to think about what they are doing – sometimes called 'unconscious competence'. What effective readers do subconsciously is to vary the reading **strategies** they use according to **what** it is that they are reading and **why** they are reading it. The examples given in the box below will give you the general idea.

## Your reading strategies

How do you read each of the following?

- The telephone directory to find a telephone number.
- A magazine whilst sitting in a reception area waiting for an appointment.
- A chapter in a textbook from which you have to make some notes.
- A newspaper to find out about how your favourite player performed in a match.
- A manufacturer's guarantee for an item of equipment that no longer works.
- A novel you have taken with you to read on a journey.

What that exercise was intended to demonstrate to you is that there is more to being a skilled reader than you perhaps realized and that with a bit of thought and effort you can make explicit the reading strategies you habitually deploy. Once you have done that, you are then in a position to begin to develop the strategies you need to use so that you can make more effective use of them. You can make a start by practising the reading skills set out in the box below.

## Improving your reading skills

- **Use the contents page** of a book or a report to form an impression of the information it contains and how that information is structured.
- **Make a note** of the titles of chapters and the headings given to sections, subsections and paragraphs – a quick summary of what the text is about.

- **Pay particular attention** to what is said in introductions, summaries and conclusions.
- Read a piece of text quickly, picking out key points and ideas relevant to your purpose – a speed-reading technique called **skimming**.
- Look quickly through all parts of the text in order to get an overall impression of what it is about or to locate things of particular interest to you – another method used in speed-reading known as **scanning**.
- **Ask yourself questions** whilst you are reading, eg 'What is the main argument?' 'Is this relevant?' 'What use is this information?'
- **Underline** (or **highlight**) in order to identify key points in an argument or to separate hard evidence or facts from the opinions expressed by the writer.
- **Annotate** a section of text, eg by inserting headings/sub-headings, writing comments in the margins and drawing lines to connect the text to diagrams and tables.
- **Summarize** the key points made by the writer in a chapter of a book or section in a report.
- **Check out** the meaning of any technical words or terms (or jargon) that you do not understand – and that affect your understanding of the text.
- Take a minute – it might be a few minutes in some instances – to **reflect** on what you have just read. In so doing ask yourself if the text has answered all your questions, if there were any passages that you found difficult to understand or if you need to reread any sections.
- **Review** what you have read as a component of the reading process – especially where extensive blocks of information (eg reports, study materials and technical articles) have to be understood and remembered. Undertake such revision within a short time of the original reading (hours rather than days).

Practising the strategies just listed will help you to become a more efficient reader, and it shouldn't take too long. Enhanced reading skills are bound to help you to assimilate information more quickly and accurately, to interpret instructions correctly and to respond appropriately – even under the time pressure you will experience at an assessment centre or a multi-assessment event. But don't leave it until the last minute – you can make a start by undertaking a review of your reading of this chapter thus far.

## Improving your listening skills

Important though reading skills are, your listening skills may prove even more important at critical times during a multi-assessment event. After all, if there is something on the page you don't understand you can only obtain clarification via the spoken word. Then you have to listen – obviously. There are so many times during an assessment centre when you need to listen carefully when people are talking in order to understand what is being said. In summary, the effectiveness of your listening skills will affect your ability to:

- respond properly to the verbal instructions you will be given at various times;
- in an interview understand the questions put to you and answer them to the best of your ability;
- in role-play and group decision-making exercises interact appropriately and constructively with the other participants.

In each case, if you misinterpret or fail to recognize the significance of what is being said, you cannot hope to answer the question or deal with the situation to the best of your ability. Remember too that you are under the pressure of being assessed. Even more so than with your reading skills, it makes excellent sense to work on polishing your listening skills. If reading skills cannot be taken for granted, listening skills certainly warrant every bit as much attention. How often do we hear the words but don't pick up their full meaning? It's the difference between plain listening and active listening.

It might seem obvious but it bears repeating: effective communication is a two-way process – you are both the transmitter of messages *to* other people and the receiver of communications *from* them. Consequently, if you don't pay attention you will not be in a position to receive and correctly decode the messages they are sending in your direction. So, because it is a two-way process, having good communication skills is not just about talking to people. It's also about listening to (and looking at) them as well, in order to interpret correctly what it is that they are saying to you – both verbally and non-verbally. That is called 'active listening'.

Because modern British society is so diverse, there is a good chance that you may be trying to communicate without the benefit of a 'common language'. Yes, of course English is prevalent in the UK but it is not necessarily everyone's first language. Consequently, in order to communicate effectively, we have to be able to do so in contexts that are culturally diverse. This means taking into account the ways in which differences in age, education, ethnicity, gender, nationality, regional origin and socio-economic background can lead to variations in the following:

- tone of voice and patterns of emphasis as means by which the flow of information is managed, meaning is clarified and emotions are expressed;
- patterns of 'taking turns' in conversation;
- ways of expressing agreement and disagreement (eg when someone says 'Yes', does it mean 'I've heard what you say' or 'I agree with what you have said'?);
- codes and conventions used for communicating politeness (or lack of it);
- means of structuring arguments and organizing information;
- how emotions are expressed – including the extent to which it is considered appropriate to express them in particular situations;
- the terminology (or jargon) used in conversation without any explanation.

From this list, it is easy to see why misunderstandings are likely to occur when two people from different 'speech communities' try to talk to each other – especially if each individual interprets what the other says from the perspective of his or her own culture. Such a situation could easily arise at an assessment centre, notably in role-play and group decision-making exercises. A good starting point for averting a possible breakdown in communication is to do some work on your listening and the closely related observation skills. Some suggestions for doing that are given in the box below.

## Improving your listening skills

- When in a garden, park or rural area make a note of the things you can hear. Then close your eyes and concentrate for a few moments on nothing else but listening. What can you now hear that you hadn't noticed before? Repeat the exercise when you are in a crowded room or in a busy part of a town or city.
- In a situation in which you are able to do so (eg a one-to-one conversation or a meeting), practise giving the speaker your full attention. Remember that 'your full attention' means *listening* carefully to what the speaker is saying, and *watching* the person closely, ie noting his or her body language.
- With regard to the latter, pay particular attention to the eyes, facial expressions, gestures and posture – in so doing try to interpret what they are 'telling' you.
- In such situations, practise maintaining your concentration – avoid 'switching off' if you disagree with what is being said, think that you have heard it all before or believe that you already know what is coming next.
- Indicate to the speaker that you are listening by giving positive feedback – in so doing explore both verbal communication (eg 'I agree with what you're suggesting') and non-verbal (eg eye contact and a nod of the head).
- Check out with the speaker the accuracy of the information that you *think* you have heard, eg 'Am I right in thinking that...?' In so doing, gauge the reactions (both verbal and non-verbal) to what you have said.

- At an appropriate point, summarize what you see as being the main points the speaker has made (eg 'So the main points to remember are...').
- Record a broadcast discussion (radio or television) and use it to practise your listening skills. As an exercise, concentrate your attention on the opinions expressed by different speakers or, in the case of a video recording, focus your attention on the speaker's (or speakers') body language.

Time spent on activities such as those just listed should help you to sensitize yourself to the importance of your listening and related observation skills. Improving these skills should enhance your ability to interpret correctly what other people are saying. This helps you in all sorts of ways – in group discussion, role-play activities, interviews and even feedback when you have not been successful. That said, as with the other skills you are seeking to develop, it will take time and effort on your part. So, don't delay – make a start as soon as you can.

## Preparing for an assessment centre: some final advice

The advice we gave you in the individual chapters focused by necessity on particular aspects of assessment centres and multi-assessment events. Now we pull together and synthesize that advice into advice of a more general nature:

- Start your preparation as early as you can. Working on your reading skills, practising for psychometric tests, improving your listening and speaking skills and developing your role-play and interview techniques all take time.
- To succeed at an assessment centre or multi-assessment event you will probably have to achieve a high standard

across the range of tests and exercises. It follows that you cannot afford to ignore any one of them.

- To further your development across a wide range of competencies use the **Appendix** to undertake an audit of your strengths and weaknesses.
- Convert the outcomes of that self-evaluation into a personal development action plan that seeks to build on your strengths and addresses in specific ways where you could do better.
- With any action plan it always helps to be clear about what you are trying to achieve (your goals) and to set yourself some realistic targets. With the latter, always lay down achievable deadlines.
- When it comes to implementing your action plan, don't try to do everything in a rush and all at once. It may be better at times to concentrate your attention on one or two items to the exclusion of others, eg on developing your reading skills or working on your listening skills. Much will depend on such matters as how well you manage your time and how you learn best.
- Keep a record (perhaps in the form of a reflective diary) of what you have done and what you think you have learnt. Use it from time to time to review your progress, eg by comparing the goals and targets in your action plan with what you think you have achieved. Adjust your plans in the light of the outcomes.
- If your self-evaluation suggests that you have weaknesses in certain areas that you cannot address by yourself, seek guidance from the appropriate places. Your local tertiary college is an obvious starting point, but help is also available from other sources, which can be accessed via the web.
- Enlist the support of others, eg to help you practise for role-play exercises and interviews.

## Summary

In this chapter we have provided you with constructive guidance on developing your reading and listening skills. Neither should ever be taken for granted, especially listening skills. We also offered some final thoughts on how best to go about preparing yourself for attending an assessment centre or multi-assessment event.

9

# After an assessment centre: how to achieve future success

The **aim** of this concluding chapter is to provide you with guidance on: obtaining feedback on how you performed at an assessment centre or multi-assessment event; evaluating your experience; and using the outcomes of self-review as the basis for initiating a programme of personal development and, through that, achieving future success.

## Seeking feedback from others

As a participant at an assessment centre it may well be that you are not given a decision about whether or not you have been selected before you leave – that will come later in the form of a phone call or a letter. However, what you should expect is to be given some form of feedback on how well you performed. Indeed a short debriefing session may well have been structured into the programme (see **Figure 1.2**) for precisely this purpose.

If you find that the assessors do not intend to offer feedback to you before you depart, you should be prepared to take the initiative and ask for it. Their willingness to respond positively will no doubt be conditioned by a number of factors, including the manner in which you make your request and how busy they are with other commitments at the time. To get off on the right foot, it would not go amiss to begin by offering your thanks for the experiences afforded to you at the assessment centre. An opening along these lines may well be seized on as an opportunity to open up a dialogue with you that would be beneficial to both sides – as professionals, the assessors should be just as keen as you are to receive some evaluative feedback on the event. If, however, both the time and circumstances are unfavourable, you would be well advised to indicate that you appreciate their situation and ask if it would be possible for you to telephone at a mutually convenient time.

If you have already been told that you have not been selected, you should try to overcome your immediate sense of disappointment. Instead, adopt a positive frame of mind in which you think of this setback as the starting point for your preparation for the next assessment event you are invited to attend. After all, success, or lack of it, is always relative – you may have performed as well as you thought you could and to the best of your ability, but still lost out to another candidate for reasons best known to the assessors.

## Feedback process

It is important to remember with feedback that it takes two sides to make it effective – the giving and the receiving. If the assessor is skilled at giving feedback he or she ought to give you a clear indication of:

- how well you performed overall;
- how well you coped with the individual assessment exercises;

- what you need to work on in order to improve your performance;
- what your developmental priorities should be if you are to succeed at your next assessment centre.

If the assessors do not volunteer useful feedback of this kind, it is up to you to use your oral communication and interpersonal skills to extract it from them.

So much for the 'giving': what about the 'receiving'? This can be tough. There are no easy ways to receive adverse criticism. Our advice is to:

- Listen carefully to the feedback – even if you find it uncomfortable.
- Try not to be too defensive by immediately rejecting what has been said or arguing with the person providing the feedback.
- Make a mental note of points of disagreement or questions you wish to ask so that you can check them out later if there is an opportunity to do so.
- Make sure that you understand the feedback before you respond to it – a useful and effective way of doing this is to paraphrase or summarize what the person has said in order to check that you have understood.
- Ask questions to clarify what has been said if you do not understand the feedback you have been given.
- Ask for feedback on specific aspects of your performance that you would find useful.
- Afterwards, reflect on the feedback you have been given and on the basis of your evaluation decide how best you can use it.

Finally, we offer three pieces of advice. First, however 'sore' and disappointed you may feel, resist the temptation to 'shoot the messenger' – don't complain to some higher authority about the person giving the feedback. It does happen occasionally, but it is invariably counter-productive. Second, try to avoid 'selective hearing syndrome', as illustrated in the following conversation:

*First person:* You are the most intelligent, humorous, compassionate, witty and considerate person I have EVER met. I prefer your company to that of anyone else even though you are a bit moody sometimes.

*Second person:* What do you mean by 'a bit moody sometimes'?

Third, remember to thank the person who has gone to the trouble of providing you with feedback – it does no harm to show your appreciation for what he or she has tried to do.

## Self-review – evaluating your assessment centre experience

Your aim should now be to reflect on your assessment centre experience in the light of the feedback you have been given, with a view to devising an action plan for your personal development. The purpose of that plan should be to increase your chances of success at the next assessment centre or multi-assessment event you attend. In devising that plan you would be well advised to:

- Reflect systematically on your experiences and the feedback you received.
- Record the key points to emerge from that reflection.
- Use the outcomes as the basis for identifying the action you need to take in order to improve your future performance at an assessment centre.

## Developing a self-improvement action plan

The framework shown in **Figure 9.1** is intended to help you to drive your self-review process. What you are looking to arrive at is a set of action points that have materialized through a process of structured reflection. You will of course need to turn those action points into a coherent action plan in which you set yourself some targets. With regard to those targets our advice would be to make them **SMART**, ie:

**S** specific
**M** manageable
**A** appropriate and achievable
**R** relevant, realistic and recorded
**T** time limited.

Effectively, you need to be as systematic and diligent in devising an action plan for your own self-improvement as you were in reflecting on your experiences. If you are capable of doing that and translating your plan into constructive action you are bound to increase your chances of success next time you attend an assessment centre or multi-assessment event. You will also have learnt some important lessons about managing your own continuous development and furthering your lifelong learning – attributes that are increasingly valued by employers.

## Summary

In this concluding chapter we have provided you with guidance on: obtaining feedback on how you performed at an assessment centre or multi-assessment event; evaluating your experience; and using the outcomes of self-review as the basis for initiating a programme of personal development and, through that, achieving future success.

| Assessment centre experiences | Evaluation feedback | Action to be taken |
|---|---|---|
| Planning and preparation | Eg: Assessor said I was caught out too often (eg in the interview) by lack of background knowledge about the organization and details of work involved. | Eg: Make sure that I have studied details of the organization (eg web page) and that I am familiar with the job specification. |
| Ability test(s) | Eg: Assessor said that I lost marks by failing to complete both tests; I felt I could have answered the questions correctly had I not run out of time. | Eg: Use practice tests to become more accustomed to working under time pressure. |
| Personality questionnaire | | |
| Emotional intelligence questionnaire | | |
| Group discussion exercise | | |
| Presentation exercise | | |
| Case study: in-tray/in-box exercise | | |
| Role-play exercise | | |
| Interview | | |

**Figure 9.1** Assessment centre self-review framework

# Appendix: Auditing your skills

> *Success in the knowledge economy comes to those who know themselves – their strengths, their values, and how best to perform.*
>
> (Drucker, P, Managing yourself, *Harvard Business Review*, March–April, pp 65–71, 1999)

Look at each of the statements in the tables that follow and try to decide how competent you are at each of the skills. Record your decision by placing a ✓ in the appropriate box in the table. In each case use the following scale:

**1** = I am good at this
**2** = I can do this most of the time, but with some difficulty
**3** = I need to work on this in order to improve.

**Table A.1** Oral communication skills

| | | 1 | 2 | 3 |
|---|---|---|---|---|
| a | In discussion I know when to listen and when to speak. | | | |
| b | When I speak I can do so in a clear, concise and confident manner. | | | |
| c | When making presentations I know how to structure and organize what I have to say. | | | |
| d | When making presentations I can pitch what I am saying to suit the audience. | | | |
| e | When making presentations and in discussion I am able to deal effectively with questions. | | | |
| f | I am able to elicit information from others in different situations through effective use of questioning. | | | |
| g | I know when it is better to talk directly to someone, or to communicate with them via the telephone, e-mail, or in writing. | | | |
| h | In one-to-one and group discussion I am able to deal effectively with difficult people. | | | |
| i | In one-to-one situations and in groups I am able to identify and take account of people's 'hidden agendas'. | | | |

**Table A.2** Written communication skills

| | | 1 | 2 | 3 |
|---|---|---|---|---|
| **a** | I can write in order to achieve my purpose (eg to present ideas or advance an argument). | | | |
| **b** | I select and use the appropriate form of document (eg letter, fax, memo, essay or report). | | | |
| **c** | I include sufficient information to achieve my purpose (eg present enough information to support my conclusions). | | | |
| **d** | I keep to the main point, elaborating only where necessary. | | | |
| **e** | I link information and ideas in an organized way. | | | |
| **f** | I use paragraphs, headings and sub-headings to structure my writing. | | | |
| **g** | I vary the vocabulary and structure of sentences according to my purpose and the audience. | | | |
| **h** | I 'pitch' the message to suit the audience. | | | |
| **i** | I proof-read what I have written in order to ensure that standard conventions of spelling, grammar and punctuation have been used correctly. | | | |

**Table A.3** Listening skills

| | | 1 | 2 | 3 |
|---|---|---|---|---|
| a | I maintain eye contact with those with whom I am talking. | | | |
| b | I focus on what is said, as well as on how things are being said. | | | |
| c | I can shut out distractions when listening to someone. | | | |
| d | I don't make notes immediately – I ask for clarification and then make notes. | | | |
| e | I ask questions to make sure that I have understood what has been said. | | | |
| f | I listen carefully (and keep my eyes open) for clues as to what messages might be hidden behind what is being said. | | | |
| g | I take careful note of how others are listening to what is being said and by whom. | | | |

**Table A.4** Reading skills

| | | 1 | 2 | 3 |
|---|---|---|---|---|
| a | I study the Contents pages to determine what the reading matter is about and how it is structured. | | | |
| b | I am able to summarize an item of text. | | | |
| c | I am able to use introductions, summaries and conclusions to find out what the writer is trying to achieve. | | | |
| d | I am able to scan text in order to quickly find out what I need to know. | | | |
| e | I can quickly skim-read text in order to get the gist of what the writer has to say. | | | |
| f | I am able to use techniques such as underlining, highlighting, and annotation to enhance my understanding of text. | | | |
| g | I take time to reflect on what I have been reading in order to ensure that I have understood it to the best of my ability. | | | |
| h | I systematically review what I have read and the methods I have been using. | | | |

**Table A.5** Numeracy

| | | 1 | 2 | 3 |
|---|---|---|---|---|
| a | I can prepare accurate estimates by avoiding errors and omissions in collecting, recording and calculating data. | | | |
| b | I know when it is acceptable to estimate and when I need to make exact calculations. | | | |
| c | I can recognize dubious statistical arguments/presentations of evidence. | | | |
| d | I can convert numerical data from one format to another. | | | |
| e | I can construct and use charts, diagrams and graphs (eg pie charts, histograms and scatter diagrams). | | | |
| f | I can use quantitative evidence to support an argument as and when necessary. | | | |
| g | I understand the limitations of statistical data. | | | |
| h | I can check mathematical solutions for their accuracy and plausibility. | | | |

**Table A.6** Information technology (IT)

| | | 1 | 2 | 3 |
|---|---|---|---|---|
| **a** | I can make effective use of a wide range of software packages. | | | |
| **b** | I can combine information drawn from different sources into a single document including text, images, graphs and charts. | | | |
| **c** | I can create automated routines to aid the efficient processing of information. | | | |
| **d** | I can make efficient use of e-mail, including the sending of attachments. | | | |
| **e** | I can extract and make effective use of information obtained via the Internet. | | | |
| **f** | I can make presentations using IT packages such as PowerPoint. | | | |
| **g** | I can access information from databases, CD-ROMs and the Internet. | | | |
| **h** | I can store information using directories and folders, and can retrieve it as and when required. | | | |
| **i** | I can evaluate the effectiveness of the procedures I use and introduce modifications to improve my performance. | | | |

**Table A.7** Planning and prioritizing work

| | | 1 | 2 | 3 |
|---|---|---|---|---|
| a | I prepare for and plan my work well in advance. | | | |
| b | I have contingency plans I can use in the event of possible setbacks. | | | |
| c | I meet deadlines and generally get the job done on time. | | | |
| d | I keep the flow of my work moving even when required to multi-task. | | | |
| e | When delegating work to others I make sure that I use their time effectively. | | | |
| f | I bring my projects to a conclusion on time. | | | |
| g | I am capable of managing several things simultaneously (eg working, studying, pursuing my personal outside interests). | | | |

**Table A.8** Adapting to and managing change

| | | 1 | 2 | 3 |
|---|---|---|---|---|
| a | I adopt a positive attitude when asked 'What would you do if…?'. | | | |
| b | I can readily adapt to changes which impact upon my personal life and work. | | | |
| c | I can produce ideas and solutions to problems created by change. | | | |
| d | I can see when changes need to be made and can take appropriate action. | | | |
| e | When faced with unforeseen changes I can respond by thinking on my feet and without panicking. | | | |

**Table A.9** Making decisions

| | | 1 | 2 | 3 |
|---|---|---|---|---|
| a | Whilst being willing to consult others, I take personal responsibility for my decisions. | | | |
| b | I make decisions by or before a 'crunch' date or time. | | | |
| c | I can allow my judgements to be modified by new information. | | | |
| d | I do not hesitate to make decisions in situations of ambiguity and uncertainty. | | | |
| e | I seek different kinds and sources of information so as to make better judgements. | | | |
| f | I evaluate the consequences of taking alternative decisions. | | | |
| g | I will reconsider a decision if a case is made for doing so. | | | |
| h | I refer decisions upwards when it is appropriate to do so. | | | |

**Table A.10** Getting on with people

| | | 1 | 2 | 3 |
|---|---|---|---|---|
| a | I am able to challenge alternative viewpoints calmly and rationally. | | | |
| b | I am able to work cooperatively with others from various functions and backgrounds. | | | |
| c | I am willing to concede, in the interests of team goals and harmony. | | | |
| d | I am aware of the impact I can have on others. | | | |
| e | I recognize the need to build constructive relationships with people. | | | |
| f | I actively encourage two-way communication. | | | |
| g | I make all the people I work with feel respected and valued. | | | |

**Table A.11** Influencing/negotiating

| | | 1 | 2 | 3 |
|---|---|---|---|---|
| a | When presenting my own viewpoint I convey personal commitment and belief. | | | |
| b | I put together reasoned, convincing arguments to support my positions. | | | |
| c | I anticipate possible objections and counter-arguments and respond accordingly. | | | |
| d | I assemble arguments to appeal to others' interests and concerns. | | | |

**Table A.12** Flexibility/creativity

| | | 1 | 2 | 3 |
|---|---|---|---|---|
| a | I am able to combine different viewpoints and perspectives to produce original ideas. | | | |
| b | I am able to find new and different ways to put ideas across. | | | |
| c | I keep an open mind until enough information accumulates to make me change a decision. | | | |
| d | I am prepared to act as devil's advocate in order to clarify an issue. | | | |
| e | I can adjust my viewpoint as new evidence becomes available. | | | |

**Table A.13** Problem solving

| | | 1 | 2 | 3 |
|---|---|---|---|---|
| **a** | I am aware that problems exist that have no immediate solutions. | | | |
| **b** | I am able to select and use appropriate methods to explore a problem and analyse its main features. | | | |
| **c** | I am able to establish the criteria which have to be met to show that a problem has been solved successfully. | | | |
| **d** | I am capable of generating different options for tackling a problem. | | | |
| **e** | I can analyse options and devise an action plan based on the option which has the most realistic chance of success. | | | |
| **f** | I can implement my action plan, making effective use of feedback and support from others in the process. | | | |
| **g** | I can review progress towards solving a problem and revise the approach as necessary. | | | |
| **h** | I can check whether the criteria have been met for the successful solution of a problem. | | | |
| **i** | I can review my approach to solving a problem, including whether alternative methods/options might have been more effective. | | | |

Table A.14 Improving learning and performance

| | | 1 | 2 | 3 |
|---|---|---|---|---|
| a | I routinely collect and record evidence which shows that I am learning from experience. | | | |
| b | I am capable of identifying my own strengths and weaknesses (like filling in this audit). | | | |
| c | I can set myself personal development goals which seek to build on my strengths and address my weaknesses. | | | |
| d | I am capable of devising an action plan for the achievement of these goals. | | | |
| e | I deal well with setbacks. | | | |
| f | I accept feedback on my performance without defensiveness. | | | |
| g | I am capable of responding positively to the constructive criticism of others. | | | |
| h | I can build on positive feedback. | | | |
| i | I am capable of reflecting on my experiences and using the outcomes to plan future actions. | | | |

## Notes

1. Now you have finished your skills audit what does the completed profile tell you? What are the strengths on which you can build? What could you do better? Are you satisfied that the evidence on which you have based your judgements is sufficiently comprehensive? Go back over your answers to assure yourself that you are telling the truth to yourself and are not just idly ticking boxes.
2. It is seldom good practice – if ever – to rely solely on self-evaluation, so check out the results of your audit with others who know you well.
3. Using the results of the audit, and the chapter by chapter guidance offered in this book, draw up an action plan for enhancing your everyday performance.

~~16~~ 14